BASIC COURSE
MODULE 3
SINHALA STRUCTURES

BY
BONNIE GRAHAM MacDOUGALL
with KAMINI de ABREW

FOREIGN SERVICE INSTITUTE
DEPARTMENT OF STATE

FOREIGN SERVICE INSTITUTE
BASIC COURSE SERIES
Edited by
MARIANNE LEHR ADAMS

Email jacobeligoodson1@outlook.com with
order number for free mp3 audio of the text

FOREWORD

This is the third volume of Basic Sinhala, a course for the beginning student which is presented in three modules:

I   Beginning Signs and Letters
II   General Conversation
III Sinhala Structures

Many individuals and institutions, both here and in Sri Lanka, were instrumental in bringing this series of lessons to its present form. Acknowledgments are made in the foreword to the second module, General Conversation.

This module is intended as a reference manual on Sinhala structures which will supplement and expand on the brief notes which appear in module II, General Conversation. At the present time most of the students for whom Basic Sinhala has been prepared begin the study of Sinhala after they arrive in Sri Lanka. The organization of language instruction there differs in some important ways from that at the Foreign Service Institute. Generally all aspects of course presentation and design are the responsibility of the classroom teacher. The teacher presents the structural analysis of the language to the students, writes and presents special materials as required by individual needs, and conducts the actual audio-lingual instruction. The number of students involved in basic Sinhala courses at any given time is limited to a small official staff, but the specific goals and needs of the students, ranging from the language of agricultural development to that of cultural affairs to that necessary simply to answer the Embassy phones in the evening, are so disparate as to place demands on the classroom teacher way out of proportion to their numbers. This module has been revised in consultation with the classroom teachers at the Embassy with the following objectives in mind: (1) to simplify the task of presenting Sinhala structures in class and thereby to free the teacher for other work; (2) to enable the teacher to write additional materials on new topics as required by student needs without constructing an entirely new course, and (3) to assist the student in assigned homework and review.

Grammar is considered a dry topic by some and a fearsome one by many others. For either audience we hope these pages have been relieved somewhat by the pictures of other kinds of "Sinhala structures" which were generously provided to us by the Ceylon Tourist Board.

Bonnie Graham MacDougall
Ithaca, New York
April 1979

iii

TABLE OF CONTENTS

THE KANTAKA CHAITIYA AT MIHINTALE

I   THE SOUND SYSTEM

Sinhala has twenty-five consonants which are arranged below according to point and manner of articulation.

		lab.	den.	alv.	ret.	pal.	vel.	glot.
Stops	voiceless	p	t		T	c	k	
	voiced	b	d		D	j	g	
	pre-nasalized	m̌b	ňd		ňD		ňg	
Spirants		f	s			ś		h
Nasals		m	n			ñ		
Liquids				l				
				r				
Semivowels		w				y		

The following vowels occur in Sinhala both short and long.

i		u
e	ə	o
æ		a

As the chart on the preceding page should suggest, the sound system of Sinhala is not sharply divergent from that of English. In fact, many, if not most of the sounds in Sinhala can be identified with those in English without obstructing communication, although this should not be taken to mean that Sinhala speakers will regard the pronunciation as accentless.

The similarities between the two languages notwithstanding, there are some areas of the Sinhala sound system which are not reminiscent of English and to which the learner will have to pay particular attention. They are treated below.

1.   The <u>contrast</u> <u>between</u> <u>dental</u> <u>and</u> <u>retroflex</u> <u>stops</u>.

The Sinhala dental stops /t/ and /d/ are articulated against the tooth ridge. The retroflex stops are articulated in a more retracted position. English <u>t</u> and <u>d</u> are normally identified with the Sinhala retroflex stops rather than with the dental ones. Examples are abundant in numerous English loan words in Sinhala. Examples:

Sinhala	English
මැජ්ස්ටික්	Majestic (name of a Colombo theater)
ජෙටිය	jetty
හෝටලේ	hotel
කෝට්	coats
ගුැත්ඩ්පාස්	Grandpass, a municipal ward in Colombo

2.   The <u>contrast</u> <u>between</u> <u>nasal</u> + <u>consonant</u> <u>and</u> <u>nasalized</u> <u>consonant</u>.

As the chart on the preceding page shows, Sinhala has four pre-nasalized consonants (m̆b, n̆d, n̆D and n̆g) which contrast with the following consonant clusters: mb, nd, nD and ng. Examples of the contrast appear below.

කොළඹ	Colombo	කොලොම්බුව	wooden stool
කඳ	tree trunk	කන්ද	hill
මඩල	circle	මණ්ඩලය	circle

2

Failure to master this contrast completely is not likely to result in embarassing bloopers, since it appears that there are not a large number of paired words with highly divergent meanings which are distinguished in this way. The contrast, however, often has grammatical significance. Singular and plural forms of the same word are sometimes distinguished in this way: for example circle/circles above.

3.   The contrast between single and doubled consonants.

In Sinhala most consonants occur both singly and doubled in the middle of words between vowels. The only exceptions are the nasalized stops, /f/, /ś/, /h/ and /r/ which occur only singly. The contrast occurs only medially.   It does not appear either in word initial or in word final position.

Mastry of this contrast is of great importance for the learner. There are a large number of paired words which are distinguished in this way. (An extensive list of examples appears in General Conversation pp. 5-7).   This contrast is important not simply because the list of words which show it is long, but also because those words occur with high frequency in conversation. Moreover, the contrast has grammatical significance. An adjectival verb form shows single /n/, for example, whereas the infinitive form shows /nn/.   Examples are given below.

යන	going	යන්න	to go
බොන	drinking	බොන්න	to drink
කන	eating	කන්න	to eat

4.   Sinhala vowels and syllable-timed rhythm.

English has a system of stresses which marks differences in word meanings (insight, incite), and which also determines the quality of some vowels and times the rhythm of the sentence. In the English stress-timed rhythm the time required to proceed from one main stress to another is roughly equal regardless of the number of intervening syllables. Vowels in those syllables which intervene between primary stresses are likely to be "reduced".   Sinhala does not have this system. Rhythm is syllable timed, that is, syllables are roughly equal in length. Vowels should be pronounced with "full value", that is, as spelled. For example, මෙහේ, 'here', not මහේ . කොලොම්බුව, 'stool'; not කලම්බුව , and so forth.

3

SEATED BUDDHA AT THE GAL VIHARA, POLONNARUWA, 12TH CENTURY

II   THE GRAMMATICAL SYSTEM

1.   Nouns

1.1.   Introduction

　　　Many of the distinctions made in the Sinhala nominal system will seem logical and familiar to the speaker of English. As in English, the noun is marked for number, that is as either singular or plural. Nouns are also marked for definiteness, a grammatical category which is handled in English with preceding articles, i.e., the book (definite), a book (indefinite).

　　　There are two broad categories of nouns in Sinhala, animate and inanimate. The former refers to people and animals and the latter includes all other nouns. Certain kinds of relationships between nouns and verbs are marked in Sinhala with case endings. Subjects of sentences are generally in the direct case, an un-marked form of the noun which is the one entered in dictionaries. Other case categories include the dative (the form for the indirect object), genitive (the possessive form) and the instrumental. Nouns in Sinhala can be categorized according to the form of the case endings. The basic division is between animate and inanimate nouns. Inanimate nouns are further subdivided into four classes.

1.2.   Sample paradigms of Sinhala nouns

　　　The generalizations which appear in 1.1 are illustrated below with representative forms. The inflected forms of the Sinhala noun are illustrated with five paradigms, each of which represents a major class of nouns.

A.   මහත්තයා   the gentleman

singular definite forms

direct	මහත්තයා	the gentleman
dative	මහත්තයාට	to the gentleman
genitive	මහත්තයාගේ	of the gentleman
instrumental	මහත්තයාගෙන්	by the gentleman

singular indefinite forms

direct	මහත්තයෙක්	a gentleman
dative	මහත්තයෙකුට	to a gentleman
genitive	මහත්තයෙකුගේ	of a gentleman
instrumental	මහත්තයෙකුගෙත්	by a gentleman

plural forms

direct	මහත්තුරු	gentlemen
dative	මහත්තුරුන්ට	to gentlemen
genitive	මහත්තුරුන්ගේ	of gentlemen
instrumental	මහත්තුරුන්ගෙත්	by gentlemen

B.   පොත   the book

singular definite forms

direct	පොත	the book
dative	පොතට	to the book
genitive	පොතේ	of the book
instrumental	පොතෙත්	by the book

singular indefinite forms

direct	පොතක්	a book
dative	පොතකට	to a book
genitive	පොතක	of a book
instrumental	පොතකින්	by a book

6

plural forms

direct	පොත්	books
dative	පොත්වලට	to books
genitive	පොත්වල	of books
instrumental	පොත්වලින්	by books

C.   බස් එක   the bus

singular definite forms

direct	බස් එක	the bus
dative	බස් එකට	to the bus
genitive	බස් එකේ	of the bus
instrumental	බස් එකෙන්	by the bus

singular indefinite forms

direct	බස් එකක්	a bus
dative	බස් එකකට	to a bus
genitive	බස් එකක	of a bus
instrumental	බස් එකකින්	by a bus

plural forms

direct	බස්	busses
dative	බස්වලට	to busses
genitive	බස්වල	of busses
instrumental	බස්වලින්	by busses

7

THE KIRI VIHARA, POLONNARUWA, 12th CENTURY

D.   හෝටලේ   the hotel (sometimes also spelled හෝටලය, the base for the indefinite forms -- see below.)

<u>singular</u> <u>definite</u> <u>forms</u>

direct	හෝටලේ	the hotel
dative	හෝටලේට	to the hotel
genitive	හෝටලේ	of the hotel
instrumental	හෝටලෙන්	by the hotel

<u>singular</u> <u>indefinite</u> <u>forms</u>

direct	හෝටලයක්	a hotel
dative	හෝටලයකට	to a hotel
genitive	හෝටලයක	of a hotel
instrumental	හෝටලයකින්	by a hotel

<u>plural</u> <u>forms</u>

direct	හෝටල්	hotels
dative	හෝටල්වලට	to hotels
genitive	හෝටල්වල	of hotels
instrumental	හෝටල්වලින්	by hotels

E. ගෙදර   house

<u>singular</u> <u>definite</u> <u>forms</u>

direct	ගෙදර	the house
dative	ගෙදරට	to the house
genitive	ගෙදර	of the house
instrumental	ගෙදරින්	by the house

singular indefinite forms

direct	ගෙදරක්	a house
dative	ගෙදරකට	to a house
genitive	ගෙදරක	of a house
instrumental	ගෙදරකින්	by a house

plural forms

direct	ගෙදරවල්	houses
dative	ගෙදරවල්වලට	to houses
genitive	ගෙදරවල්වල	of houses
instrumental	ගෙදරවල්වලින්	by houses

The noun forms given above are representative ones, that is, the rest of the nouns in Sinhala are declined like one of those given above. All animate nouns show endings like 'the gentleman', in paradigm A. As for inanimate nouns, in order to know which one of the remaining classes a particular noun belongs to, one must know the direct definite singular form and the genitive definite singular form. These forms vary according to class. In order to predict all the forms of a particular noun, one must know these two forms and the direct plural form as well. Directions for forming other forms from these basic ones are given below.

1.21 A nouns: nouns declined like මහත්තයා 'the gentleman'

Nouns belonging to the class illustrated by මහත්තයා, 'the gentleman', are all animate nouns. The following are examples of nouns which belong to this particular class.

මහත්තයා	the gentleman
නංගි	the younger sister
අම්මා	the mother
පිතිසා	the man

10

Important characteristics of A nouns

a. The genitive case ending is ගේ

b. The instrumental case ending is ගෙන්

Examples of A nouns in sentences

මහත්තයා නුවරට යනවා.	The gentleman is going to Kandy.
අම්මා කොළඹ ඉන්නවා.	Mother lives in Colombo.
තාත්තා ආණ්ඩුවේ වැඩ කරනවා.	Father works for the government.
අම්මාගේ අයියා ගෙදර ගියා.	Mother's elder brother went home.

Further information on the formation of A noun case forms appears
in 1.3.

1.22   B nouns: nouns declined like පොත 'the book'.

This class of inanimate nouns is the most important one
because it has the largest membership. One can usually assume that
a noun ending in අ belongs to class B. Examples:

පාර	the road
ලංකාව	Sri Lanka
අමෙරිකාව	America
කුල්ල	the winnowing basket
ලාම්පුව	the lamp
කට	the mouth

Important characteristics of B nouns

a. The direct definite singular ends in අ

b. The genitive definite singular ends in ේ

c. The instrumental definite singular ends in ේන්

11

THE RUVANVELI DAGABA AT ANURADHAPURA, 2nd CENTURY B.C.

Examples of B nouns in sentences:

මහත්තයා ආවේ අමෙරිකාවෙන්.	The gentleman came from America.
මම ඉපදුනේ ලංකාවේ.	I was born in Sri Lanka.
මේ පාර යන්නේ නුවරට.	This road goes to Kandy.

1.23 C nouns: nouns declined like බස් එක 'the bus'.

Nouns which belong to this class end in එක . Many words from English have been borrowed into Sinhala as class C nouns. The following Sinhala nouns belong to class C:

කාර් එක	the car
ටෙලිෆෝන් එක	the telephone
ෆොටෝ එක	the photo
ලිෆ්ට් එක	the elevator

Important characteristics of C nouns

a. The direct definite singular form ends in   එක.

b. The plural direct form can be formed from the direct definite singular form by removing එක. Examples

බස් එක	singular direct definite form
බස්	plural direct

c. The instrumental definite singular ends in එකෙන් Example:

බස් එකෙන්	by the bus

d. The genitive definite singular ends in එකේ Example:

බස් එකේ	of the bus

13

Examples of C nouns in sentences

බස් එකෙන් යන්න පුලුවන් ද?　　　　　Can (you) go by bus?

ටෝච් එකක් තියෙනවා ද?　　　　　　　Is there a flashlight?

මහත්තයා ළඟ ටිකට් එකක් තියෙනවා ද?　Do you have a ticket, sir?

1.24 D nouns: nouns declined like හෝටලේ 'the hotel'

Important characteristics of D nouns

　　　　The direct definite singular form and the genitive definite singular form of D nouns end in ි . The dictionary entry form given in () below is generally spelled with -අය , however.

උත්තරේ (උත්තරය)　　　　　　　the answer

කාලේ (කාලය)　　　　　　　　the time, period

මේසේ (මේසය)　　　　　　　　the table

Examples of D nouns in sentences

අපි ආවේ හෝටලෙන්.　　　　　　We came from the hotel.

ගොයම් කපන කාලෙට ගෑනු කුඹුරට　At paddy cutting time, women take

කෑම ගෙනියනවා.　　　　　　　food to the field.

1.25 E nouns: nouns declined like ගෙදර 'the house'

　　　　In the direct definite singular, all E nouns end in අ.
The following Sinhala nouns belong to class E:

ගෙදර　　　　　　　　　　　　the house

කොළඹ　　　　　　　　　　　　Colombo

මැද　　　　　　　　　　　　　the middle

හවස　　　　　　　　　　　　　the afternoon

14

Important characteristics of E nouns

a. The direct definite singular and the genitive definite sin-
    gular forms end in අ.

b. The instrumental definite singular ends in ඉන්.

c. The class has a very limited membership. Most nouns with
    direct case endings in අ belong to class B.

Examples of E nouns in sentences

මහත්තයා ගෙදර ඉන්නවා ද?   Is the gentleman in the house?

හෙට මම කොළඹට යනවා.   I am going to Colombo tomorrow.

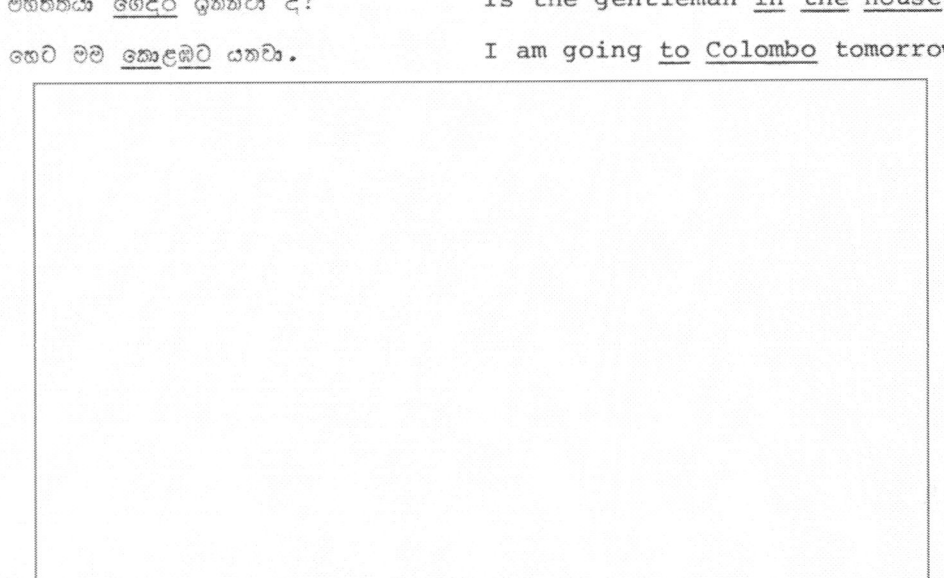

THE RUVANVELI DAGABA FROM A DISTANCE WITH THE JETAVANARAMAYA
DAGABA (3rd CENTURY A.D.) TO THE RIGHT. FOREGROUND, THE NUWARA
WEWA, THE LARGEST TANK IN ANURADHAPURA (3000 ACRES).

1.3   The cases

1.31   The direct case

     Direct case forms may be singular indefinite, singular defi-
nite or plural. Thus, පොත, 'the book', පොතක්, 'a book', and
පොත්, 'books', are all direct case forms.

15

Subjects of verbs are in the direct case. For example:

පාරක් තියෙනවා.	There is <u>a road</u>.
මම ඉන්නේ නුවර.	<u>I</u> live in Kandy.
තාත්තා ඉන්දියාවට යනවා.	<u>Father</u> is going to India.
මහත්තයා ආවේ අමෙරිකාවෙන්.	<u>The gentleman</u> came from America.

Direct objects of verbs are also usually in the direct case.

මහත්තයා ලියුම් එවනවා.	The gentleman <u>sends letters</u>.
මහත්තයා ලියුමක් එවනවා.	The gentleman is sending <u>a letter</u>.
මහත්තයා ලියුම එවනවා.	The gentleman is sending <u>the letter</u>.

The direct definite singular form is the one a Sinhala gives
when asked for the translation of an English word. It is also
the form entered in dictionaries.

1.32   The <u>dative</u> <u>case</u>

The dative case ending is ට . Dative case forms may be
singular definite, singular indefinite or plural. The dative
case in Sinhala most often translates the English 'to somewhere,
something or someone.' Thus, a dative case form is equatable
with what is sometimes called the indirect object. Examples:

මම <u>අමෙරිකාවට</u> යනවා.	I am going <u>to America</u>.
මම අර ගමට ගියා.	I went <u>to that village</u>.
මම මල්ලිට සල්ලි දුන්නා.	I gave money <u>to younger brother</u>.
මම ගමකට යනවා.	I am going <u>to a village</u>.
මම හේන්වලට යනවා.	I am going <u>to the chenas</u>.

1.321   Use

Sometimes dative case forms translate into English as indirect objects, as in the examples above. Sometimes they equate
with other structures, as in the examples below.

For instance, with the verb ඕනැ 'want', the actor is in the dative case. Examples:

මට අමෙරිකාවට යන්න ඕනෑ.	I want to go to America.
මට ටිකට් එකක් ගන්න ඕනෑ.	I want to get a ticket.
මහත්තයාට තේ බොන්න ඕනෑ.	The gentleman wants to drink tea.

The actors in sentences with පුලුවනි 'can' and බෑ 'cannot', are also in the dative case. Examples:

මට සිංහල කතාකරන්න පුලුවනි.	I can speak Sinhala.
මට ඉංග්‍රීසි කියවන්න පුලුවනි.	I can read English.
මහත්තයාට කාර් එලවන්න පුලුවනි.	The gentleman can drive cars.
මල්ලිට ඉන්දියාවට යන්න පුලුවනි.	Younger brother can go to India.
මට සිංහල කතාකරන්න බෑ.	I cannot speak Sinhala.
මහත්තයාට වැඩ කරන්න බෑ.	The gentleman cannot work.
නංගිට අමෙරිකාවට යන්න බෑ.	Younger sister cannot go to America.

The dative case form is used in construction with the verbs ඉන්නවා and තියෙනවා 'be', to produce the meaning 'have' or 'have to'. Examples:

මට සල්ලි තියෙනවා.	I have money (lit., there is money to me.).
මහත්තයාට බල්ලෙක් ඉන්නවා.	The gentleman has a dog (lit., there is a dog to the gentleman).

With a dependent infinitive තියෙනවා takes on the meaning 'have to'. Examples:

මට ගෙදර යන්න තියෙනවා.	I have to go home
මට කාර් එකෙන් යන්න තියෙනවා.	I have to go by car.
මට හාල් ගන්න තියෙනවා.	I have to buy rice.
මහත්තයාට වැඩ කරන්න තියෙනවා.	The gentleman has to work.

LANKATILAKA IMAGE HOUSE, POLONNARUWA, 12th CENTURY

1.322   Formation of dative case forms

In the singular definite, the dative case ending is added to the direct definite singular form. Thus, ගෙදර + ට = ගෙදරට පාර + ට = පාරට , පුතා + ට = පුතාට.
This rule applies to both animate and inanimate nouns. The formula for forming the dative indefinite singular for inanimate nouns is direct indefinite singular form + අ + ට.

For animate nouns the formula is: direct indefinite singular form + ු + ට.

Examples:

ගෙදරක්	a house	ගෙදරකට	to a house
පාරක්	a road	පාරකට	to a road
බල්ලෙක්	a dog	බල්ලෙකුට	to a dog
මිනිහෙක්	a man	මිනිහෙකුට	to a man

In the plural the dative case ending is added to the <u>plural stem</u>. For inanimate nouns the plural stem is identical with the genitive plural (see 1.3323). For example, එළවළුවල + ට = එළවළුවලට 'to the vegetables'; ගෙදරවල්වල + ට = ගෙදරවල්වලට 'to the houses'. You can look at the formation of the dative plural of inanimate nouns in another way: the ending වලට is added to the direct plural form. Thus, ගෙදරවල් + වලට = ගෙදරවල්වලට 'to the houses', and so forth.

With animate nouns, the dative case ending is also added to the plural stem. If the direct plural form ends in ලා , the plural stem is identical with the direct plural. Thus:

plural stem	dative plural	
නංගිලා	නංගිලාට	to the younger sisters
මල්ලිලා	මල්ලිලාට	to the younger brothers

If the direct plural form of an animate noun ends in ඕ , the stem ends in අන් . If it ends in ු , the stem ends in උන් .

Look at the examples below.

19

direct plural		plural stem	plural dative
මහත්තුරු	gentlemen	මහත්තුරුන්	මහත්තුරුන්ට
කුකුලෝ	chickens	කුකුලන්	කුකුලන්ට
කොල්ලෝ	boys	කොල්ලන්	කොල්ලන්ට
බල්ලෝ	dogs	බල්ලන්	බල්ලන්ට
අරගොල්ලෝ	those people	අරගොල්ලන්	අරගොල්ලන්ට

The rules above will generate dative forms of all classes. Review the sample paradigms and look at the dative case forms which appear.

1.33 The genitive case
1.331 Use

Nouns in the genitive case often show possession.   Examples:

මගේ පොත.	My book.
තාත්තාගේ දුව.	Father's daughter.
මහත්තයාගේ රස්සාව.	The gentlemen's job.
පොතේ කවරය.	The cover of the book.
ගෙදර දොර.	The door of the house.

In some instances they show location and translate the English 'on or in something'. Examples:

මම වැඩ කරන්නේ ආණ්ඩුවේ.	I work in the government.
මහත්තයා වැඩ කරන්නේ හෝටලේ.	The gentleman works in the hotel.
මම ඉන්නේ ගෙදරක.	I live in a house.

1.332 Formation of genitive case forms

Definite singular forms of the genitive must be memorized. For some classes of nouns they are predictable from the direct singular form, and for other classes they are not.

20

ARADHANAGALA AT MIHINTALE

1.3321 <u>Genitive</u> <u>definite</u> <u>singular</u> <u>forms</u>.

In the genitive definite singular, class A nouns take the ending
ගේ . This ending is added to the direct definite singular form.
Examples:

<u>direct</u> <u>definite</u> <u>singular</u>		<u>genitive</u> <u>definite</u> <u>singular</u>
මහත්තයා	gentleman	මහත්තයාගේ
දුව	daughter	දුවගේ
තංගි	younger sister	තංගිගේ

For nouns ending in   අ   one cannot determine the class by looking
at the direct definite singular. Both B and E nouns have direct
definite singular forms in   අ . If the noun is class E like ගෙදර
'house', the genitive definite singular form is identical with
the direct. If the noun is class B like පොත 'the book', the
genitive definite singular ends in   ේ , i.e.,   පොතේ.

For class C nouns like බස් එක 'the bus', the genitive definite
singular form is predictable. It ends in   ේ , i.e., බස් එකේ .

If the noun is class D like හෝටලේ 'the hotel', the genitive
definite singular form is also predictable. It is identical
with the direct.

1.3322 <u>Genitive</u> <u>indefinite</u> <u>singular</u> <u>forms</u>

For inanimate nouns the formula is <u>indefinite</u> <u>direct</u> <u>form</u> plus අ.

<u>direct</u> <u>indefinite</u>		<u>genitive</u> <u>indefinite</u>	
පොතක්	a book	පොතක	of a book
හෝටලයක්	a hotel	හෝටලයක	of a hotel
ගෙදරක්	a house	ගෙදරක	of a house
පාරක්	a road	පාරක	of a road

The formula for the genitive indefinite form of animate nouns is
<u>indefinite</u> <u>direct</u> <u>form</u> + උගේ . Examples:

<u>direct</u> <u>indefinite</u>		<u>genitive</u> <u>indefinite</u>	
බල්ලෙක්	a dog	බල්ලෙකුගේ	of a dog
කොල්ලෙක්	a boy	කොල්ලෙකුගේ	of a boy
බළලෙක්	a cat	බළලෙකුගේ	of a cat

22

1.3323 Genitive plural forms

The formula for genitive plural forms of inanimate
nouns is direct plural form + වල . Examples:

direct plural		genitive plural	
එළවළු	vegetables	එළවළුවල	of vegetables
ගෙදරවල්	houses	ගෙදරවල්වල	of houses
හේන්	chenas	හේන්වල	of chenas

The formula for the genitive plural of animate nouns is plural
stem (cf. 1.32) + ගේ . Sometimes the plural stem is identical
with the direct plural (see 1.32). For instance, in the case of
direct plurals ending in ලා :

direct plural		plural stem	plural genitive
නංගිලා	younger sisters	නංගිලා	නංගිලා ගේ
අයියලා	older brothers	අයියලා	අයියලාගේ

Often however, the plural stem is not identical with any case form.
For example:

direct plural		plural stem	plural genitive
මහත්තුරු	gentlemen	මහත්තුරුන්	මහත්තුරුන්ගේ
බල්ලෝ	dogs	බල්ලන්	බල්ලන්ගේ
කොල්ලෝ	boys	කොල්ලන්	කොල්ලන්ගේ

With උ and ඕ plurals, note above in 1.32 that the formula for
the plural stem is direct plural form, minus the final vowel plus
either උන් or අන් .   If the direct plural ends in උ , add උන්
for the stem; if it ends in ඕ , add අන් .

1.34   The instrumental case

1.341 Use

Instrumental case forms are generally translated into English as
'by, with or from something.' Appropriate translations vary.

මම කෝච්චියෙන් ගියා.   I went by train.

මේ බඩුවලින් සමහරක් මගේ.   Some of these goods are mine.

එයා ආවේ අමෙරිකාවෙන්.   He came from America.

1.342 Formation of instrumental case forms.

1.3421 Instrumental definite singular forms.

For inanimate nouns the instrumental forms end in either ඉන් or එන් .
Examples:

definite singular:	direct		instrumental
Class B nouns	පොත	book	පොතෙන්
Class C nouns	කාර් එක	car	කාර් එකෙන්
Class D nouns	මේසේ	table	මේසෙන්
Class E nouns	ගෙදර	house	ගෙදරින්

Look back at the sample paradigms given above in 1.2.

The formula for the instrumental definite singular form of animate
nouns is direct definite singular form plus ගෙන් .   Examples:

	direct		instrumental
	එයා	he	එයාගෙන්
	කෙල්ල	girl	කෙල්ලගෙන්

1.3422 Instrumental indefinite singular forms.

For inanimate nouns the formula is direct indefinite singular form
plus ඉන් .   Examples:

indefinite singular:	direct		instrumental
	පොතක්	a book	පොතකින්
	ගෙදරක්	a house	ගෙදරකින්

For animate nouns the formula is direct indefinite singular form
plus උගෙන් .   Examples:

24

<u>direct indefinite singular</u>   <u>instrumental indefinite singular</u>

පුතෙක්	a son	පුතෙකුගෙන්
දුවෙක්	a daughter	දුවෙකුගෙන්

1.3423 <u>Instrumental plural forms</u>

With inanimate nouns the formula for the instrumental plural is <u>plural direct form</u> + වලින් . Examples:

<u>direct plural</u>		<u>instrumental plural</u>
ගෙදරවල්	houses	ගෙදරවල්වලින්
පොත්	books	පොත්වලින්
හේන්	chenas	හේන්වලින්

The formula for the instrumental plural of animate nouns is <u>plural stem</u> + ගෙන් . Examples:

<u>direct plural</u>		<u>plural stem</u>	<u>instrumental plural</u>
මහත්තුරු	gentlemen	මහත්තුරුන්	මහත්තුරුන්ගෙන්
නංගිලා	younger sisters	නංගිලා	නංගිලාගෙන්

1.4 <u>Definite and indefinite forms of the noun</u>

Definiteness and indefiniteness are marked only in the singular The definite forms such as පාර, 'road', බස් එක 'bus', and නගුල 'plow', may be translated as 'road, bus, plow' or 'the road, the bus, the plow'. Indefinite forms such as පාරක් , බස් එකක් , and නගුලක් , are best translated as 'a road, a bus, a plow'.

The direct indefinite of inanimate nouns ends in අක් . Examples:

<u>direct indefinite form</u>

ගෙදරක්	a house
ගමක්	a village
රටක්	a country

The direct indefinite of animate nouns ends in එක් . Examples:

DAMBULLA ROCK TEMPLE, 1st CENTURY B.C.

<u>direct</u> <u>indefinite</u> <u>form</u>

බල්ලෙක්   a dog

පුතෙක්   a son

Formulas for the formation of all definite and indefinite case
forms have appeared in 1.3.

1.5 <u>Animate</u> <u>and</u> <u>inanimate</u> <u>nouns</u>: <u>agreement</u>

     As previously noted in 1.2, animate nouns are declined
differently than those which are inanimate. There are also
differences in agreement, some of which are given below.

1.51 තියෙනවා and ඉන්නවා 'be'.

Examples:

මල්ලිලා ඉන්නවා.   There are younger brothers.

කාර් තියෙනවා.   There are cars.

The verbs තියෙනවා and ඉන්නවා both mean 'be'. Forms of the verb
තියෙනවා may only be used with subjects which are inanimate.
ඉන්නවා   is used only with animate subjects.

1.52 <u>Animate</u> <u>and</u> <u>inanimate</u> <u>nouns</u> <u>and</u> <u>quantity</u>.

     There are animate numerals and inanimate numerals. Animate
numerals either modify or are substituted for animate nouns.
Inanimate numerals either modify or are substituted for inanimate
nouns. Examples:

මහත්තුරු තුන් දෙනෙක් ඉන්නවා.   There are <u>three</u> gentlemen.

කාර් තුනක් තියෙනවා.   There are <u>three</u> cars.

තුන් දෙනෙක් ඉන්නවා.   There are <u>three</u> (animate)

තුනක් තියෙනවා.   There are <u>three</u> (inanimate).

27

මහත්තයෙක්	a gentleman	ගෙදරක්	a house
මහත්තුරු දෙත්තෙක්	2 gentlemen	ගෙදරවල් දෙතක්	2 houses
මහත්තුරු තුන් දෙතෙක්	3 gentlemen	ගෙදරවල් තුනක්	3 houses
මහත්තුරු හතර දෙතෙක්	4 gentlemen	ගෙදරවල් හතරක්	4 houses
මහත්තුරු පස් දෙතෙක්	5 gentlemen	ගෙදරවල් පහක්	5 houses
මහත්තුරු හය දෙතෙක්	6 gentlemen	ගෙදරවල් හයක්	6 houses

Other numeral forms appear in 6.

ENTRANCE TO DAMBULLA ROCK TEMPLES

2.   Verbs

2.1 Basic classes.   Sinhala verbs fall into three main classes:

1. Verbs with a stem vowel අ.   Example: කපනවා   'cut'

2. Verbs with a stem vowel එ.   Example: වැටෙනවා   'fall'

3. Verbs with a stem vowel ඉ.   Example: බඳිනවා   'bind'

The verb forms given above are simple present tense forms.   The
simple present tense form is the one entered in most Sinhala
dictionaries.

The formula for the stem of a Sinhala verb is simple present tense
form minus නවා .   The vowel on the end of this stem is called the
stem vowel.   For most verbs all forms are predictable once the
stem vowel is known although there is a small list of "irregular
verbs" (which regrettably for the learner are those of highest
frequency).   The first vowel in the stem is called the root vowel.
Make a note of the stem and root vowels in the verb forms given
above.

2.2 Present tense forms

2.21 The simple present tense or නවා form.   Examples:

මම ගෙදර යනවා.   I am going home.

ගල් හතරක් තියෙනවා.   There are four stones.

මල්ලි මෙහාට එනවා.   Younger brother is coming in this
                                 direction.

අම්මා බත් උයනවා.   Mother cooks rice.

ඉස්කෝලේ මහත්තයා සිංහල උගන්නනවා.   The schoolmaster teaches Sinhala.

2.22 The emphatic present tense or න්නේ form.

මම යන්නේ ගෙදර.   It is home that I am going.

මම කන්නේ මස්.   It is meat that I am eating.

යන්නේ කොහේ ද?   Where are (you) going?

කරන්නේ මොනවා ද?   What are (you) doing?

DAMBULLA ROCK TEMPLES

Both the තවා and the ත්තේ forms are present tense forms. Usually
the use of the ත්තේ form means that <u>some</u> <u>item</u> <u>other</u> <u>than</u> <u>the</u> <u>verb</u>
in the sentence is singled out for emphasis. Examples:

a. කන්තෝරුව අටට අරිනවා.   The office opens at 8:00.

b. කන්තෝරුව අරින්නේ අටට.   It is at 8:00 that the office
                                 opens.

a. එයා හවස ආපහු එනවා.   He is coming back in the evening.

b. එයා ආපහු එන්නේ හවස.   It is in the evening that he is
                                 coming back.

In the "b" sentences above, the words අටට and හවස are singled
out for emphasis.   In the "a" sentences no particular item is
singled out for emphasis.

2.23 <u>The</u> <u>question</u> <u>marker</u> <u>and</u> <u>present</u> <u>tense</u> <u>forms</u>

     The question marker ද may follow the තවා form of the verb.
Examples:

   මහත්තයා ගෙදර යනවා ද?   Is the gentleman going home?

   වතුර බොනවා ද?   Are (you) drinking water?

   සල්ලි තියෙනවා ද?   Is there money?

But the question marker ද never follows the ත්තේ form of the verb.
It always goes after some other item in the sentence, usually the
emphasized one.   Examples?

   එයා ගෙදර එන්නේ හවස ද?   Is it in the evening that he is
                                 coming home?

   කන්තෝරුව වහන්නේ අටට ද?   Is it at 8:00 that the office
                                 closes?

   එයා බොන්නේ වතුර ද?   Is it water that he is drinking?

31

THE TEMPLE AT ISURUMUNIYA, 3rd CENTURY B.C.

2.24 Negatives with the present tense.
2.241 The negative of තවා .

Affirmative	මම බොනවා.	I drink.
Negative	මම බොන්නේ නෑ.	I don't drink.
Affirmative	මහත්තයා යනවා.	The gentleman goes.
Negative	මහත්තයා යන්නේ නෑ.	The gentleman doesn't go.
Affirmative	මම බිත්තර කනවා.	I eat eggs.
Negative	මම බිත්තර කන්නේ නෑ.	I don't eat eggs.
Affirmative	මම වැඩ කරනවා.	I work.
Negative	මම වැඩ කරන්නේ නෑ.	I don't work.

The formula for negating the තවා form is න්නේ form + නෑ . Two
exceptions are the verbs තියෙනවා 'be' (inanimate) and ඉන්නවා 'be'
(animate). Their negative forms are simply නෑ.

2.242 Negating emphatic sentences with නෙමෙයි 'is not'.

Affirmative	මම යන්නේ කඩේට.	It is to the store that I am going.
Negative	මම යන්නේ කඩේට නෙමෙයි.	It is not to the store that I am going.
Affirmative	මම ඉන්නේ අමෙරිකාවේ.	I live in America.
Negative	මම ඉන්නේ අමෙරිකාවේ නෙමෙයි.	It is not in America that I live.
Affirmative	මම බොන්නේ වතුර.	It is water that I drink.
Negative	මම බොන්නේ වතුර නෙමෙයි.	It is not water that I drink.
Affirmative	මම කන්නේ බිත්තර.	It is eggs that I eat.
Negative	මම කන්නේ බිත්තර නෙමෙයි.	It is not eggs that I eat.

33

In emphatic sentences such as the ones above, the item singled out for emphasis follows the verb. This type of sentence is negated by adding නෙමෙයි,'is nòt/are not', after the emphasized item.

2.25 <u>Negative/interrogative</u> <u>sentences</u>.

Sentences with නෙමෙයි, 'is not/are not' may be made interrogative by adding the question marker ද in sentence final position. Sentences with නෑ such as those in 2.241 are also negated with the question marker ද . නෑ plus ද becomes නැද්ද . Examples:

මහත්තයා යන්තේ නෑ.	The gentleman doesn't go.
මහත්තයා යන්තේ නැද්ද?	Doesn't the gentleman go?
මම වැඩ කරන්තේ නෑ.	I don't work.
මම වැඩ කරන්තේ නැද්ද?	Don't I work?

2.26 <u>Present</u> <u>forms</u> <u>with</u> <u>question</u> <u>words</u>.

Question words such as මොකක්, 'what',මොනවා, 'what', කොහේ , where', and others occur in sentences with the න්තේ form of the verb. With the exception of ඇයි , 'why', which stands alone, these words are immediately followed by the question marker ද . Examples:

මහත්තයා යන්තේ කොහොම ද?	How are you going, sir?
නෝනා මහත්තයා කරන්තේ මොනවා ද?	What are you doing, madam?
ඒකට කියන්තේ මොකද්ද (=මොකක් ද)?	What do you call that?
මහත්තයා සිංදු කියන්තේ මොකද?	Why do you sing, sir?
ඇයි යන්තේ, මහත්තයා?	Why are you going, sir?
නෝනා මහත්තයා කොහේ ද ඉන්තේ?	Where are you living, madam?

When present verbs in the negative occur in construction with question words they take the shape -න්තේ form plus නැත්තේ. Examples:

ඇයි යන්තේ නැත්තේ?/යන්තේ නැත්තේ මොකද?	Why don't you go?
මොනවා ද කරන්තේ නැත්තේ?	What aren't you doing?

2.27 The emphatic negative form

The න්නේ form plus නැත්තේ which has appeared above with question words is an emphatic negative form of the verb.   Compare:

මම යන්නේ කඩේට.   It is to the store that I am
                                   going.

මම යන්නේ නැත්තේ කඩේට   It is not to the store that I
                                   am going.

කන්තෝරුව අරින්නේ අටට.   It is at 8:00 that the office
                                   opens.

කන්තෝරුව අරින්නේ නැත්තේ අටට.   It is not at 8:00 that the office
                                   opens.

See section 2.242 for sentences which although different in structure from those above are roughly similar in meaning.

2.28 Rapid speech forms

Before a following නැ and some other negative forms based on it such as නැත්තේ , the න්නේ form of the verb becomes න් in rapid speech. Examples:

Optimal signal	එයා වැඩ කරන්නේ නෑ.	He doesn't work.
Rapid speech form	එයා වැඩ කරන් නෑ.	He doesn't work.
Optimal signal	එයා යන්නේ නැත්තේ මොකද?	Why doesn't he go?
Rapid speech form	එයා යන් නැත්තේ මොකද?	Why doesn't he go?

35

2.29 <u>This</u> <u>thing</u> <u>is</u> <u>mine</u>./ <u>That</u> <u>is</u> <u>a</u> <u>loaf</u> <u>of</u> <u>bread</u>. Equational
sentences.

Sentences of the form x is y lack verbs in Sinhala. Examples.

    මේක මගේ.   This thing is mine.

    අර පාන් ගෙඩියක්.   That is a loaf of bread.

    කාර් එක අලුත්.   The car is new.

    කමිසය හොඳ එකක් ද?   Is the shirt a good one?

2.291 <u>Negation</u>

When the word in the "y" slot is an adjective, it is negated
with නෑ .   Examples:

    කාර් එක අලුත් නෑ.   The car is not new.

    වැඩ ලේසි නෑ.   The work is not easy.

When the word in the "y" slot is a noun or pronoun, it is negated
with තෙමෙයි . Examples.

    අර පාන් ගෙඩියක් තෙමෙයි.   That is not a loaf of bread.

    කමිසය හොඳ එකක් තෙමෙයි.   The shirt is not a good one.

    මේක මගේ තෙමෙයි.   This thing is not mine.

2.3   The <u>present</u> <u>verbal</u> <u>adjective</u> <u>or</u> න <u>form</u>

2.31 <u>Use</u> <u>of</u> <u>the</u> න <u>form</u>

The න form precedes the noun it modifies. Examples:

    යන මිනිස්සු   <u>Going</u> men (or men who are going)

    ගොයම් කපන කාලේ   Paddy <u>cutting</u> time.

    සිංහල ඉගෙනගන්න ළමයි.   Sinhala <u>learning</u> children (or
                                  children who are learning Sinhala)

    මම කියවන පොත   The book I am <u>reading</u>.

ආණ්ඩුව කරන වැඩ.

The work which the government is doing.

Note that constructions with the present verbal adjective often equate with English relative clauses.

2.32 Formation of the න form

The න form is made up of the verb stem + න . Examples:

simple present form		verb stem	න form
යනවා	go	ය -	යන
බොනවා	drink	බො -	බොන
කපනවා	cut	කප -	කපන
බදිනවා	fry	බදි -	බදින

2.33 Forms based on the present verbal adjective

2.331 The කොට , 'when', form.

2.3311 Use.

The කොට form is used to convey the meaning 'When (I) am doing something.' The action in the කොට clause is simultaneous with the action in the main clause. Examples:

මම උදේ කෑම කනකොට, පත්තර කියවනවා.

I read the papers when I am eating breakfast.

මම නානකොට, සිංදු කියනවා.

When I bathe, I sing.

2.3312 Formation of the කොට form.

The කොට form is made up of the present verbal adjective plus කොට.

present verbal adjective		කොට form
යන	go	යනකොට
බොන	drink	බොනකොට
කපන	cut	කපනකොට
බදින	fry	බදිනකොට

2.332   The කන් 'till' form.

2.3321   Use

The කන් form is used to convey the meaning 'until such an action happens.'   Examples.

අට වෙනකන්, මම වැඩ කරන්නම්.	I'll work until (it becomes) 8:00, if you like.
මහත්තයා එනකන්, ඉන්න.	Stay till the gentleman comes.
මම වැඩ ඉවර කරනකන්, එයා එන්නේ නෑ.	He isn't coming till I finish the work.

2.3322   Formation of the කන් form.

The කන් form is made up of the present verbal adjective plus කන් Examples:

present verbal adjective		කන් form
වෙන	become	වෙනකන්
යන	go	යනකන්
එන	come	එනකන්
කරන	do	කරනකන්

2.3333   Stylistic variation

There is a කල් form which is a variant of the කන් form.   Example:

එයා එනකල්, ඉන්න.	Wait till he comes.

38

2.333 The present verbal adjective with නිසා , 'because'.

2.3331 Use

The present verbal adjective occurs in construction with නිසා, 'because', and has the meaning 'because (subject) does such and such.'   Examples:

එයා වැඩ කරන නිසා.	Because he is working.
මහත්තයා යන නිසා.	Because the gentleman is going.
මම උදේ කෑම කන නිසා.	Because I am eating breakfast.
මම සහල් මතින නිසා, දැන් යන්න බෑ.	I can't go now because I am measuring the rice.
මම සිංහල ඉගෙනගන්න නිසා, දැන් එන්න බෑ.	I can't come now because I am studying Sinhala.

2.3332 Related negative forms

The negative adjectival form is නැති . Negative present verbs which appear before නිසා take the form න්නේ form plus නැති . Examples:

මම යන නිසා.	Because I am going.
මම යන්නේ නැති නිසා.	Because I am not going.
මම සහල් මතින නිසා.	Because I am measuring the rice.
මම සහල් මතින්නේ නැති නිසා.	Because I am not measuring the rice.

2.3333 Dialect and stylistic variation

Another word meaning 'because' is හින්දා. It occurs in the same types of constructions as නිසා .

2.4 Past tense forms

2.41 The simple past tense form

Present	මම වැඩ කරනවා.	I work
Past	මම වැඩ කෙරුවා.	I worked

Present   මම සිංහල ඉගෙනගන්නවා.   I am learning Sinhala.

Past   මම සිංහල ඉගෙනගත්තා.   I learned Sinhala.

The simple past tense form of the verb expresses completed action. It fills slots which are similar to those filled by the simple present tense, or නවා form, i.e., it usually goes at the end of a sentence and it may be followed by the question marker ද .

2.42 The emphatic past tense form

Emphatic present   මම කන්නේ මස්.   It is meat that I am eating.

Emphatic past   මම කෑවේ මස්.   It was meat that I ate.

Emphatic present   යන්නේ කොහේ ද?   Where are you going?

Emphatic past   ගියේ කොහේ ද?   Where did you go?

The emphatic past tense form also expresses completed action. Like the emphatic present form, it is used when some item other than the verb in the sentence is singled out for emphasis. It is also used with question words. It is not followed directly by the question marker ද .

2.43 Predicting the simple past tense form from the නවා form.

Step 1: Remove the නවා suffix. This leaves the verb stem.

For example:

simple present tense form		verb stem
කපනවා	cut	කප-
කඩනවා	break	කඩ-
කොටනවා	pound	කොට-
කැපෙනවා	get cut	කැපෙ-
කැඩෙනවා	get broken	කැඩෙ-
වැටෙනවා	fall	වැටෙ-

40

THE ABHAYAGIRI DAGABA, ANURADHAPURA, 1st CENTURY B.C.

<u>simple present tense form</u>		<u>verb stem</u>
බඳිනවා	bind	බඳි-
බදිනවා	fry	බදි-

<u>Step 2</u>:   If the root vowel is අ   change it to   ඇ

          If the root vowel is ආ   change it to   ඇ

          If the root vowel is ඔ   change it to   එ

          If the root vowel is ඕ   change it to   ඒ

          If the root vowel is උ   change it to   ඉ

          If the root vowel is ඌ   change it to   ඊ

If the root vowel is ඇ , ඈ , එ , ඒ , ඉ , or ඊ, do not change it.   For example:

<u>basic stem</u>		<u>altered stem</u>
කප-	cut	කැප-
කඩ-	break	කැඩ-
කැප-	get cut	කැප-
කොට-	pound	කෙට-
සෝද-	wash	සේද-
බුර-	bark	බිර-
කහ-	scratch	කැහ-

<u>Step 3</u>:   Look at the <u>stem vowel</u>.   If the stem vowel is අ , remove it and add උවා.   Verbs with stem vowel අ are class 1 verbs. If the stem vowel is එ , remove it and add ඉයා.   Verbs with stem vowel එ are class 2 verbs.   If the stem vowel is ඉ , remove it, double the preceding consonant and add ආ.   Verbs with stem vowel ඉ are class 3 verbs.   Examples:

<u>simple present tense form</u>		<u>simple past tense form</u>
1. කපනවා	cut	කැපුවා
කඩනවා	break	කැඩුවා
කොටනවා	pound	කෙටුවා

42

simple present tense form		simple past tense form
බුරනවා	bark	බිරුවා
සෝදනවා	wash	සේදුවා
2. කැපෙනවා	get cut	කැපුනා
වැටෙනවා	fall	වැටුනා
3. බදිනවා	fry	බැද්දා
නගිනවා	climb	නැග්ගා
නැගිටිනවා	get up	නැගිට්ටා
මනිනවා	measure	මැන්නා

2.44 Irregular past tense verb forms

There is a small list of verbs for which some forms are irregular. Below is a list of high frequency verbs with irregular past tense forms.

simple present tense form		simple past tense form
ඉන්නවා	be (animate)	හිටියා
තියෙනවා	be (inanimate)	තිබුනා
වෙනවා	become	උනා
කරනවා	do	කෙරුවා
දෙනවා	give	දුන්නා
ගන්නවා	get	ගත්තා
යනවා	go	ගියා
එනවා	come	ආවා
ගේනවා	bring	ගෙනාවා
කනවා	eat	කැවා
බොනවා	drink	බිව්වා
දානවා	put, place	දැම්මා

43

LANKARAMAYA DAGABA, ANURADHAPURA, 3rd CENTURY A.D.

GUARDSTONE FROM RATNAPRASADA AT ANURADHAPURA

simple present tense form		simple past tense form
නානවා	bathe	නෑවා
ගානවා	smear	ගෑවා
සානවා	plow	සෑවා

2.45 Predicting the emphatic past tense form from the simple past tense form

The formula for deriving the emphatic past tense form from the simple past form is: replace final ආ with ඒ. Examples:

simple past form		emphatic past form
කෙරුවා	do	කෙරුවේ
හිටියා	be	හිටියේ
කැපුවා	cut	කැපුවේ
කැඩුවා	break	කැඩුවේ

2.46 Negative and interrogative past tense forms

The negative and interrogative forms of the simple and emphatic past parallel those of the present. These forms are illustrated below.

simple	මහත්තයා අටට ආවා.	The gentleman came at 8:00.
emphatic	මහත්තයා ආවේ අටට.	It was at 8:00 that the gentleman came.
simple/ neg.	මහත්තයා අටට ආවේ නෑ.	The gentleman didn't come at 8:00.
emphatic/ neg.	මහත්තයා ආවේ නැත්තේ අටට.	It wasn't at 8:00 that the gentleman came.
simple/?	මහත්තයා අටට ආවා ද?	Did the gentleman come at 8:00?
emphatic/?	මහත්තයා ආවේ අටට ද?	Was it at 8:00 that the gentleman came?

simple/ neg./?	මහත්තයා අටට ආවේ නැද්ද?	Didn't the gentleman come at 8:00?
emphatic/ neg./?	මහත්තයා ආවේ නැත්තේ අටට ද?	Wasn't it at 8:00 that the gentleman came?

2.47 Dialect variation

Alternant past tense forms of three common verbs appear below.

simple present		A simple past	B simple past
අහනවා	ask	ඇහුවා	ඇහැව්වා
ගහනවා	hit	ගැහුවා	ගැහැව්වා
වහනවා	close	වැහුවා	වැහැව්වා

Both variants may be heard in the speech of educated speakers,
although variant A is preferable.

Most other variants of past tense forms are non-standard. They
include බුන්නා for බිව්වා , 'drank', හිබ්බා ,for හිටියා , 'was', and others.
In some areas of the Kandyan highlands the past tenses of all
Class 1 verbs conform to a pattern other than the one which has
been set out above and show no vowel change from present to past.
Since these forms are low prestige forms, however, they occur
infrequently in conversations with non-native speakers.

2.48 Forms based on the past tense: the past verbal adjective.

2.481 Use

The past verbal adjective occurs in constructions which are similar to those in which the present verbal adjective occurs.
It precedes the noun it modifies. Examples:

මට ලැබුන විසා එක .	The visa I <u>obtained</u>.
මම ඉපදුන ගම.	The village where I was <u>born</u>.
කැඩුන මුට්ටි.	<u>Broken</u> pots.

2.482 Formation of the past verbal adjective form.

The past verbal adjective is formed by replacing final ආ of
the simple past tense form with අ . Examples:

47

simple past form		past verbal adjective
ගියා	go	ගිය
ආවා	come	ආව
බැලුවා	see	බැලුව
කැඩුනා	get broken	කැඩුන
බැද්දා	fry	බැද්ද

2.483 The past verbal adjective with නිසා , 'because'.

Like the present verbal adjective the past verbal adjective occurs in constructions with නිසා , 'because'. Examples:

මහත්තයා ගිය නිසා.	Because the gentleman went.
මම මුට්ටි කැඩුව නිසා.	Because I broke the pots.
මම අමෙරිකාවේ ඉපදුන නිසා.	Because I was born in America.

Examples of past tense negative forms with නිසා are given below.

මහත්තයා ගියේ නැති නිසා.	Because the gentleman didn't go.
මම මුට්ටි කැඩුවේ නැති නිසා.	Because I didn't break the pots.
මම අමෙරිකාවේ ඉපදුනේ නැති නිසා.	Because I wasn't born in America.

Note: There are some other Sinhala verb forms which are derived from the past but which are not discussed in this section. They include the 'when' form and the 'even if' forms which are taken up in sections 2.8 and 2.9.

2.5   The Infinitive Form

2.51   Use

2.511 The infinitive form is used as the request form:

ඉඳගන්න.	Please sit down.
ගෙදර යන්න.	Please go home.
කෑම කන්න.	Please eat.

Request forms are negated by adding the word එපා .

කෑගහන්න එපා.	You shouldn't shout.
ගෙදර යන්න එපා.	Please don't go home.
වතුර බොන්න එපා.	Don't drink the water.

2.512 Infinitives may be the objects of other verbs:

මම නාන්න යනවා.	I am going to bathe.
මම කෑම කන්න එනවා.	I am coming to eat.
මට කෑම කන්න ඕනෑ නෑ.	I don't want to eat.
වතුර බොන්න බෑ.	Can't drink water.

**2.513 When the infinitive is followed by the question marker ද ,
it has the meaning "Should (I) do something?."**

මම මෙහෙම ලියන්න ද?	Should I write like this?
හෙට යන්න ද?	Should I go tomorrow?

2.52   Formation of the Infinitive Form

The formula for the infinitive form is <u>verb stem</u> plus න්න . Some
dialects have variants with න්ඩ and න්ට .   Examples:

Verb stem		Infinitive
ය–	go	යන්න (යන්ඩ, යන්ට)
එ–	come	එන්න (එන්ඩ, එන්ට)
කා–	eat	කන්න (කන්ඩ, කන්ට)
ගේ–	bring	ගේන්න (ගේන්ඩ, ගේන්ට)
දෙ–	give	දෙන්න (දෙන්ඩ, දෙන්ට)
කප–	cut	කපන්න (කපන්ඩ, කපන්ට)
කර–	do	කරන්න (කරන්ඩ, කරන්ට)
කොට	pound	කොටන්න (කොටන්ඩ, කොටන්ට)

49

2.6   The participle

2.61   Use

මම කෑම කාලා ගෙදර ගියා.

Having eaten, I went home. (I ate and went home)

කුඹුර හාලා පොර දාන්න.

Having plowed the field, put on fertilizer. (Plow the field and put on fertilizer)

මම ලියුමක් ලියලා තැපැල් කන්තෝරුවට ගියා.

Having written a letter, I went to the post office. (I wrote a letter and went to the post office)

THE RANKOT VIHARA, POLONNARUWA, 12th CENTURY

මම සල්ලි දීලා බඩු ගත්තා.	<u>Having given</u> the money, I got the goods. (I gave the money and got the goods)
කඩේ <u>වහලා</u> මුදලාලි නුවර ගියා.	<u>Having closed</u> the shop, the shopkeeper went to Kandy. (The shopkeeper closed the shop and went to Kandy)

In English, events are often sequenced with <u>and</u>. For example:

> I went <u>and</u> got it.
>
> He took a bath <u>and</u> went to bed.
>
> I am going to the store <u>and</u> buy some fruit.
>
> Flour the fish <u>and</u> fry it.

It is also possible to say

> Having gone, I got it.
>
> Having taken a bath, I went to bed.
>
> Having gone to the store, I'll buy some fruit.
>
> Having floured the fish, fry it.

Although the second renditions are less frequent in American English and may seem somewhat awkward, they literally translate the forms which appear in Sinhala. In Sinhala sometimes several events are sequenced in this fashion. For example:

මම කාලා, නාලා, ගෙදර ගිහිල්ලා, නිදාගත්ත ගියා.	Having eaten, having bathed, having gone home, I went to bed. (I ate, bathed, went home and went to bed)

This "having" form is called the participle. The participle may also be joined with forms of the verb තියෙනවා 'be', to form perfect tenses. For example:

මම ඒ චිත්‍රපටිය <u>දැකලා</u> තියෙනවා.	I have <u>seen</u> that movie.
එයා අමෙරිකාවට <u>ගිහින්</u> තියෙනවා.	He has <u>gone</u> to America.
මම ඒ චිත්‍රපටිය <u>දැකලා</u> තිබුනා.	I had <u>seen</u> that movie.
එයා අමෙරිකාවට <u>ගිහින්</u> තිබුනා.	He had <u>gone</u> to America.

51

THE ROCK TEMPLE AT ISURUMUNIYA

2.611 <u>Perfect</u> forms

2.6111 <u>Present</u> <u>perfect</u> <u>forms</u>

The participle plus තියෙනවා , 'be', has the meaning 'have done something.' Examples:

මම අමෙරිකාවට ගිහිල්ලා <u>තියෙනවා</u>.   I <u>have</u> <u>gone</u> to America.

මම කිරි බත් <u>කාලා</u> <u>තියෙනවා</u>.   I <u>have</u> <u>eaten</u> milk rice.

මම පොත් දෙකක් ලියලා <u>තියෙනවා</u>.   I <u>have</u> <u>written</u> two books.

These forms are present perfect forms.

2.6112 <u>Past</u> <u>perfect</u> <u>forms</u>

The participle plus තිබුනා , 'be(past)', has the meaning 'had done something.' Examples:

මම අමෙරිකාවට ගිහිල්ලා තිබුනා.   I <u>had</u> <u>gone</u> to America.

මම කිරි බත් <u>කාලා</u> තිබුනා.   I <u>had</u> <u>eaten</u> milk rice.

මම පොත් දෙකක් ලියලා තිබුනා.   I <u>had</u> <u>written</u> two books.

These forms are past perfect forms.

2.612 <u>The</u> <u>participle</u> <u>alone</u> <u>as</u> <u>a</u> <u>finite</u> <u>verb</u>.

Sometimes the participle stands alone as the finite verb. It has a perfect sense and occurs primarily with third person subjects.

කත්තෝරුව දැන් ඇරලා.   The office <u>has</u> <u>opened</u> now.

තැපැල් කත්තෝරුව දැන් වහලා.   The post office <u>has</u> <u>closed</u> now.

2.613 <u>Negative</u>, <u>interrogative</u> <u>and</u> <u>emphatic</u> <u>forms</u> <u>with</u> <u>the</u> <u>perfect</u>.

Perfect forms may be made negative, interrogative, negative/ interrogative and emphatic by applying the appropriate formulas (outlined in 2.1 and 2.3) to the auxiliary තියෙනවා , 'be'. No change is made in the participle.

2.614 <u>Durative and continuous forms with the participle.</u>

With animate subjects the participle combines with forms of the verb ඉන්නවා , 'be', to make forms which are durative (and sometimes continuous) in meaning. For example:

මම බැඳලා ඉන්නවා.	I'm married. (I'm married now and I continue to be.)
මම කොළඹ පදිංචි වෙලා හිටියා.	I was residing in Colombo. (I started living there and continued to do so for some time.)
මහත්තයා දිහා බලාගෙන ඉන්න.	Look at (in the direction of) the gentleman. (Start doing it and keep on doing it.)

KANDY LAKE WITH TEMPLE OF THE TOOTH IN DISTANCE

2.62 <u>Formation of the participle.</u>

2.621 <u>Class 1 verbs</u>

The formula for the participle for class 1 verbs is verb stem plus ලා. Examples.

<u>simple present</u>		<u>verb stem</u>	<u>participle</u>
කපනවා	cut	කප	කපලා
බලනවා	see	බල	බලලා

54

simple present		verb stem	participle
හදනවා	make	හද	හදලා
උයනවා	cook	උය	උයලා
දුවනවා	run	දුව	දුවලා

2.622 Class 2 verbs

The formula for the participle for class 2 verbs is verb stem minus ව plus ඉලා .

simple present		verb stem	participle
කැපෙනවා	get cut	කැපෙ	කැපිලා
කැඩෙනවා	get broken	කැඩෙ	කැඩිලා
තේරෙනවා	understand	තේරෙ	තේරිලා
වැටෙනවා	fall	වැටෙ	වැටිලා

2.623 Class 3 verbs

The formula for the participle for class 3 verbs is altered verb stem minus ි plus අලා .

simple present		verb stem	participle
මනිනවා	measure	මැනි	මැනලා
බදිනවා	fry	බැදි	බැදලා
මදිනවා	brush	මැදි	මැදලා

2.624 Participle forms of irregular verbs

The participle forms of the high frequency irregular verbs which appeared in 2.44 are given below. Note that not all the forms below are irregular.

simple present		participle
ඉන්නවා	be (animate)	ඉඳලා
තියෙනවා	be (inanimate)	තිබිලා

simple present		participle
වෙනවා	become	වෙලා
කරනවා	do	කරලා
දෙනවා	give	දීලා
ගන්නවා	get	අරන්
යනවා	go	ගිහිල්ලා (ගිහින්)
එනවා	come	ඇවිල්ලා (ඇවිත්)
ගේනවා	bring	ගෙනැල්ලා (ගෙනත්)
කනවා	eat	කාලා
බොනවා	drink	බීලා
දානවා	put, place	දාලා
ගානවා	smear	ගාලා
හානවා	plow	හාලා
නානවා	bathe	නාලා

2.7 The ŋ form or participial adjective

2.71 Use

Like the other adjectival forms derived from verbs which have been
discussed previously in Sinhala Structures, the ŋ form modifies
a preceding noun. Examples:

ලීවලින් හදපු ගෙදර	The house (which has been) made with wood.
බැදපු මස්	Fried meat; meat which has been fried.
මම මැනපු හාල් .	The rice I have measured.
කැපිච්ච ගස්	The trees which have been cut.

56

Like the other adjectives, the පු form occurs in construction with නිසා , 'because'. Examples:

එයා ගෙදර හදපු නිසා.	Because he has <u>built</u> the house.
අම්මා සාල් මැනපු නිසා.	Because mother has <u>measured</u> the rice.

The formula for the negative of the above forms is participle plus නැති .

එයා ගෙදර හදලා නැති නිසා.	Because he <u>hasn't</u> <u>built</u> the house.
අම්මා සාල් මැනලා නැති නිසා.	Because mother <u>hasn't</u> <u>measured</u> the rice.

The participial adjective also figures in the formation of a 'when' form which is discussed below in 2.8

2.72 Formation

2.721 Class 1 verbs.

The formula for the පු form of Class 1 verbs is: participle form minus ලා plus පු . Examples:

participle		පු form
කපලා	cut	කපු
කඩලා	break	කඩපු
හදලා	make, build	හදපු
බලලා	see	බලපු

2.722 Class 2 verbs.

The formula for the පු form of Class 2 verbs is: participle form minus ලා plus වුණ . Examples:

participle		පු form
වැටිලා	fall	වැටිච්ච
කැපිලා	get cut	කැපිච්ච
කැඩිලා	get broken	කැඩිච්ච

57

BUDUNUVAGALE

2.723 Class 3 verbs.

The formula for the පු form of Class 3 verbs is: participle form
minus ලා plus පු . Examples:

participle		පු form
නැගලා	climb	නැගපු
බැදලා	fry	බැදපු
මැනලා	measure	මැනපු
මැදලා	brush	මැදපු

2.724 Irregular verbs

පු forms for the high frequency verbs which show irregularities
in numerous forms are given below.

simple present form		පු form
ඉන්නවා	be (animate)	හිටපු
තියෙනවා	be (inanimate)	තිබිච්ච
වෙනවා	become	වෙච්ච
කරනවා	do	කරපු
දෙනවා	give	දීපු
ගන්නවා	get	අරගත්ත
යනවා	go	ගිය
එනවා	come	ආපු
ගේනවා	bring	ගෙනා පු
කනවා	eat	කාපු
බොනවා	drink	බීපු
දානවා	put, place	දාපු
ගානවා	smear	ගාපු
සානවා	plow	සාපු
නානවා	bathe	නාපු

2.8 The 'when' forms

2.81 Use

One 'when' form, the කොට form has been discussed above in
2.331. It contrasts in meaning with another 'when' form, the
ම form. Examples:

a මම රෙදි සෝදනකොට, සබන් පාවිච්චි   When I wash clothes, I use soap.
  කරනවා.

b මම රෙදි සේදුවම, අත් රතු වෙනවා.   When I wash clothes (that is,
                                           after I have done so), my hands
                                           get red.

c මම ලංකාවට යනකොට, අහස්යන්ත්‍රාවෙන්   When I go to Sri Lanka, I'll go
  යනවා.   by airplane.

d මම ලංකාවට ගියම, කෘෂිකර්ම   When I go to Sri Lanka, I'll work
  දෙපාර්තමේන්තුවේ වැඩ කරනවා.   for the Department of Agriculture.

With ම forms of the verb, the action in the 'when' clause
precedes the action in the second clause. For example, in
sentence a above, 'When I wash clothes, my hands get red', the
meaning is that the hands do not get red until after the clothes
are washed. By contrast in sentence b, 'When I wash clothes,
I use soap', the actions are simultaneous, that is, soap is
being used in the process of washing the clothes. Hence the
කොට form is appropriate in the 'when' clause (see section 2.331
for a detailed discussion).

2.82 Formation of the ම form.

The formula for the ම form is simple past tense form plus ම .

simple past		ම form
ගියා	go	ගියාම
ආවා	come	ආවාම
බැද්දා	fry	බැද්දාම
කැපුවා	cut	කැපුවාම
කෙරුවා	do	කෙරුවාම

60

2.83 Dialect variation

In the speech of some speakers the formula for the ම form is as
follows: past verbal adjective plus හම . Examples:

past verbal adjective		ම form
ගිය	go	ගියහම
ආව	come	ආවහම
කැඩුව	break	කැඩුවහම
කැපුව	cut	කැපුවහම
කෙරුව	do	කෙරුවහම

2.84 An additional 'when' form.

An additional 'when' form is built on the participial adjective
and it differs little in meaning from the ම forms described above.
The formula for this form is: participial adjective (ප form)
plus හම.

participial adjective (ප) form.		derived ම form.
ආප	come	ආපහම
කරප	do	කරපහම
වැටිච්ච	fall	වැටිච්චහම
බැදප	fry	බැදපහම

2.9 The 'if' forms

There are a number of forms and constructions in Sinhala which
equate with the English 'if (I) do something.' Two types of
equivalents are discussed below.

2.91 A conditional form of the verb.

හෙට වැස්සොත්, අපට පොලොන්නරුවට යන්න බෑ.	If it rains tomorrow, we can't go to Polonnaruwa.

ඔයා මේ කෑම කෑවොත්, අසනීප වෙනවා.   If you were to eat this food,
                                     you would become sick.

The 'if' forms in the sentences above are conditional forms of
the verb.

The formula for the conditional form of the verb is: simple
past form minus ආ plus ඔත් .   Examples:

simple past		conditional
ගියා	go	ගියොත්
ආවා	come	ආවොත්
කෙරුවා	do	කෙරුවොත්
ගත්තා	take	ගත්තොත්

Another conditional form based on the present stem occurs in
Sinhala, but it is not illustrated in General Conversation because
it seems to be of low frequency in speech and therefore of minor
importance. The formula for this form is present stem plus තොත් ,
For example, මම යතොත්   , 'if I go.'

2.92 Basic forms of the verb plus නම් , 'if'.

The English 'If (I) (am) doing something', may be expressed by a
present form plus නම් , 'if'. Examples:

පොල් ගෙඩි කඩේ තියෙනවා නම්,   If there are coconuts in the shop,
මට කියන්න.   tell me.

අපි කොළඹ යනවා නම්, මම කාර්   If we go to Colombo, I'll drive
එක එලවන්නම්.   the car, if you like.

Past forms with නම් are not semantically parallel to those of the
present. They usually have the meaning 'If (I) had done something'.
Examples:

පොල් ගෙඩි කඩේ තිබුනා නම්, මම   If there had been coconuts in the
නුවර යන්නේ නෑ.   shop, I wouldn't be going to Kandy.

අපි කොළඹ ගියා නම්, මම කාර් එක   If we had gone to Colombo, I would
එලෙව්වා.   have driven the car.

SEDANT BUDDHA, POLONNARUWA

2.10 The 'even if' form

කහට තේ එකක් හදලා දුන්නත්, එයා   Even if you prepare a plain tea
බොන්නේ නෑ.   (for him), he will not drink it.

මම එයාට ලියුම් එව්වත්, එයා මට   Even if I send him letters, he will
සල්ලි දෙන්නේ නෑ.   not give me the money.

මම කහට තේ එකක් හදලා දුන්නත්,   Even though I prepared a plain tea
එයා බිව්වේ නෑ.   (for him), he would not drink it.

මම එයාට ලියුම් එව්වත්, එයා මට   Even though I sent him letters,
සල්ලි දුන්නේ නෑ.   he would not give me the money.

Examples of the 'even if' form of the verb appear above. The
formula for the 'even if' form is simple past tense form minus
ආ plus අත් .

2.11 The 'although' construction.

Examples of the 'although' construction which is very common in
most normal communication appear below. The formula for the
although construction is: simple past tense form of the verb
plus ට plus මොක ද .   මොක ද , however, may be omitted.

එයා ඉස්කෝලේ ගියාට මොක ද, එයා   Although he goes to school, he
ඉංග්‍රීසි ඉගෙනගත්තේ නෑ.   doesn't learn English.

හය දෙනාට ලෙඩ හැදුනාට මොක ද,   Although six people became ill,
කවුරුවත් මැරුනේ නෑ.   no one died.

Note that the tense of the entire sentence is determined by that
of the main clause.

2.12 First person verb forms

2.12.1 The න්නම් form.

The න්නම් form occurs only with first person subjects. It has
a consultative meaning in that it announces an intention of per-
forming an activity and at the same time requests leave to do so.
For example:

මම මහත්තයාට කියන්නම්.   I'll tell the gentleman, if you
                                        like.

The addressee generally responds as follows:

64

John   මම මහත්තයාට තියන්තම්.   I'll tell the gentleman, if you
                                     like.

Mary.   හොඳයි.   එයාට තියන්ත.   Good.   Tell him.

The formula for the formation of the න්තම් form is verb stem plus
න්තම්   .   Examples:

simple present		verb stem		form
යනවා	go	ය		යන්තම්
එනවා	come	එ		එන්තම්
කියනවා	tell	කිය		කියන්තම්
කරනවා	do	කර		කරන්තම්

2.12.2 The මු form

Whereas the න්තම්   form may occur with first person singular or
first person plural subjects, the මු form occurs only with the
first person plural. It has the meaning 'lets do something.'
The subject (අපි , 'we') may be stated or understood. Examples:

චිත්‍රපටියක් බලන්න යමු.   Let's go see a movie.

උදේ කෑම කමු.   Let's eat breakfast.

It may precede the question marker ද .

යමු ද?   Should we go?

කමු ද?   Should we eat?

The formula for the negative is නො plus a stem form of the
participle plus ඉදිමු   , 'let's stay/be.' The literal translation
is 'not having done something, let's (just) be.'   ඉදිමු is the
මු   form of ඉන්නවා, 'be.' It is irregular. Examples:

අපි නොබලා ඉදිමු.   Let's not see .

අපි නොකා ඉදිමු.   Let's not eat .

The formula for the මු form is: verb stem plus මු . Examples:

simple present		verb stem		මු form
යනවා	go	ය		යමු
බලනවා	see	බල		බලමු
කනවා	eat	ක		කමු

Two irregular forms appear below.

simple present		මු form
ගන්නවා	take, get	ගමුමු
ඉන්නවා	be	ඉදිමු

2.13 The ඊ form

The ඊ form appears with second and third person subjects, usually with the latter, and has the meaning '(he) is likely to do something.'   Examples:

මහත්තයා හවස එයි.   The gentleman is likely to come
                              in the evening.

එයා ශෝ එකට යයි.   He is likely to go to the show.

The negative of the ඊ form is similar to the negative මු form. The formula is නෙ plus a stem form of the participle plus 'ඉදියි , 'likely to stay, be.'   ඉදියි is the ඊ form of ඉන්නවා 'be'. Its form is irregular. Examples:

එයා ඒක නොබලා ඉදියි.   He is not likely to see it.

එයා නොගිහින් ඉදියි.   He is not likely to go.

The ඊ form may precede the question marker ද .

The formula for the ඊ form is: verb stem plus ඊ . Examples:

simple present		verb stem	යි form
යනවා	go	ය	යයි
එනවා	some	එ	එයි
කරනවා	do	කර	කරයි
කියනවා	say	කිය	කියයි
ඉන්නවා	be	[irregular form]	ඉඳී

The යි form has a dialect variant with වී . The rules for forming it are different, and it does not appear to be very common. Hence it is not taken up here.

2.14 Special verbs

2.14.1   කැමතියි , 'like'.

මම මේ රටට කැමතියි.	I like this country.
මම මේ එලවළුවලට කැමති නෑ.	I don't like these vegetables.
තේ බොන්න කැමති ද?	Do (you) like to drink tea?
සිංහල ඉගෙනගන්න කැමති ද?	Do (you) like to study Sinhala?

The word කැමතියි means 'like or like to'. The actor is in the direct case. If there is an object, it is in the dative case, i.e.,

මම එලවළුවලට කැමතියි.	I like vegetables.

An infinitive may also be the object of කැමතියි , i.e.,

සිනි නැතුව එයා තේ බොන්න කැමති නෑ.	He doesn't like to drink tea without sugar.

Sentences with කැමතියි may be made interrogative by adding ද.

They may be made negative by adding නෑ .

කැමතියි   may be made past by adding උනා .

67

PARAKRAMABAHU STATUE, POLONNARUWA, 12TH CENTURY

2.14.2   පුළුවනි , '<u>can</u>', <u>and</u> බෑ , '<u>cannot</u>'.

පුළුවනි , '<u>can</u>' and බෑ , '<u>can't</u>', take actors in the dative case.
Examples:

මට කොළඹ යන්ත පුළුවනි.	I can go to Colombo.
මට වැඩකරන්ත පුළුවනි.	I can work.
මට සිංහල කතාකරන්ත පුළුවනි.	I can speak Sinhala.
මට ගෙදර යන්ත බෑ.	I can't go home.
මහත්තයාට සිංහල කතාකරන්ත බෑ.	The gentleman can't speak Sinhala.

පුළුවනි normally occurs in sentence final position, as above, but
පුළුවන් may also occur there with no change in meaning.

පුළුවනි and බෑ usually occur with a dependent infinitive. Examples:

එයාට හාන්ත පුළුවනි.	He can plow.
මහත්තයාට පත්තර කියවන්ත පුළුවනි.	The gentleman can read the papers.
නෝනා මහත්තයාට මෙහාට එන්ත බෑ.	The lady can't come here.

Sentences with පුළුවනි and බෑ may be made interrogative by adding.
ද .   Before ද, පුළුවනි changes to පුළුවන් and බෑ to බැරි . Examples:

මහත්තයාට පත්තර කියවන්ත පුළුවන් ද?	Can you read the papers, sir?
තාත්තාට දොළහට ඉස්සර එන්ත බැරි ද?	Can't you come before 12:00, father?

Sentences with පුළුවනි and බෑ may be made past by adding උනා , the
past form of වෙනවා , 'become.' Examples:

ගිය ඉරිදා මට එන්ත පුළුවන් උනා.	I was able to come last Sunday.
මට මස් හොඳට උයන්ත බැරි උනා.	I was not able to cook the meat well.

2.14.3 ඕනෑ , 'want'.

ඕනෑ , 'want', takes an actor in the dative case. Examples:

මට කොල්ලුපිටිය හන්දියට යන්න ඕනෑ.   I want to go to Colpetty junction.

මට ගැහැණු ළමයි කියලා චිත්‍රපටිය   I want to see the movie called
බලන්න ඕනෑ.   Gehenu Lamay.

මට කිරි බත් කන්න ඕනෑ.   I want to eat milk rice.

Sentences with ඕනෑ may be made interrogative by adding ද .
Examples:

මහත්තයාට විසා එකක් ඕනෑ ද?   Does the gentleman want a visa?

එයාට දැන් මට ලියකියවිලි දෙන්න   Does he want to give me the docu-
ඕනෑ ද?   ments now?

They may be made negative by adding නෑ . Examples:

මහත්තයාට කිරි තේ එකක් ඕනෑ නෑ.   The gentleman doesn't want a milk
                                     tea.

එයාට ලියකියවිලි ගන්න ඕනෑ නෑ.   He doesn't want to take the
                                     documents.

They may be made past by adding උනා . Examples:

මට කෝච්චියෙන් එන්න ඕනෑ උනා.   I wanted to come by train.

මහත්තයාට ගෙදරක් හදාගන්න ඕනෑ   The gentleman wanted to build
උනා.   a house.

ඕනෑ may be preceded either by a dependent infinitive or by a
noun in the direct case.   In sentences with dependent nouns only
there is an alternate negative form with එපා .   එපා is equivalent to ඕනෑ නෑ , 'don't want' and replaces the entire phrase. Examples:
    මට කිරි එපා.   I don't want any milk, i.e.,
                                     no milk for me.

    මට දොඩම් ඉස්ම එපා.   I don't want any orange juice.

70

2.15 <u>Negatives</u> <u>in</u> <u>Sinhala</u>: <u>some</u> <u>summary</u> <u>remarks</u> <u>and</u> <u>some</u>
<u>additions</u>.

At this point most of the negative processes and words which occur
in Sinhala have been discussed in connection with the verb forms
to which they apply. They include නැ and its various forms, මැ
and its forms, එයා and තෙමේයි.   The negative තො has been mentioned
only briefly in connection with certain specific forms. A more
detailed and general treatment appears below.

<u>The</u> <u>negative</u> තො .

තො negates forms in dependent clauses such as the conditional
form of the verb:

   හෙට තොවැස්සොත්, මම පිට-   If it doesn't rain tomorrow,
   කොටුවට යනවා.   I'm going to the Pettah.

the 'even if' form:

   මම එයාට තොකිව්වත්, එයා එනවා.   Even if I don't tell him, he'll
                            come.
the ම form:
   එයා වැඩට තොගියාම, මම තරහ   When he doesn't go to work, I get
   වෙනවා.   mad.

the කොට form:
   එයා වැඩ තොකරනකොට, සෙල්ලම් When he's not working, he is
   කරනවා.   playing.

and others.

It may also negate verbal adjective forms:

   මස් තොකන මිනිස්සු බිත්තර කනවා. The people who don't eat meat
                            eat eggs.

   කොළඹ තොගිය ගෑනු අපේ කන්තෝරුවේ The women who didn't go to Colombo
   ඉන්නවා.   are in our office.

   මම තොහැදු ගෙදර   The house I haven't built.
even if they occur in other
types of constructions:

   මම ගෙදර තොහැදු නිසා.   Because I haven't built the house.

These are the important principal uses of තො .

2.16 'It seems'

The particle ද means 'it seems', and it is added to basic forms of the verb. Examples:

ලිඩෝ එකේ හොඳ චිත්‍රපටියක් පෙන්නනවා ද.	It seems there is a good movie showing at the Lido.
එයා ළඟ සල්ලි තියෙනවා ද.	He evidently has money on him.

When නෑ precedes ද it becomes නැති . Examples:

එයා ළඟ සල්ලි නැති ද.	He evidently has no money on him.
එයා තැපැල් කන්තෝරුවේ වැඩ කරන්නේ නැති ද.	It seems that he doesn't work in the post office.

ද may follow parts of speech other than verbs. For example:

එයා තැපැල් මහත්තයා ද.	They say he's the postmaster.
මහත්තයා පොහොසත් ද.	It seems that the gentleman is rich.

2.17 Relationships among verbs

2.17.1 Verbs with කරනවා , 'do', and වෙනවා , 'become'.

There are a large number of verbs with කරනවා   which are related in meaning to a similar set with වෙනවා   .   They include:

බය කරනවා	scare	බය වෙනවා	fear
අඩු කරනවා	subtract	අඩු වෙනවා	be reduced
මතක් කරනවා	remind	මතක් වෙනවා	remember
කරදර කරනවා	bother	කරදර වෙනවා	worry
ඉවර කරනවා	finish	ඉවර වෙනවා	be finished

2.17.2 Causative/non-causative sets

Causative verbs are derived from basic verbs by adding ව to the stem.   Examples:

basic verb		causative verb	
යනවා	go	යවනවා	make go, export
කරනවා	do	කරවනවා	cause to do
කඩනවා	break	කඩවනවා	cause to break
කනවා	eat	කවනවා	cause to eat, feed

The following verbs also stand in a causative/non causative relationship, even though the initial consonants differ:

බොනවා	drink	පොවනවා	cause to drink, feed

Other types of causatives involve other changes from the basic form:

බහිනවා	descend	බස්සනවා	let (someone) down, drop off.
ගේනවා	bring	ගෙන්වනවා	import
දන්නවා	know	දන්වනවා	make known

2.173 Active and passive

Some sets of verbs are active/passive. Generally, the active verb belongs to class 1 and the passive verb to class 2. Examples:

active		passive	
කපනවා	cut	කැපෙනවා	be cut
කරනවා	do	කෙරෙනවා	be done
මරනවා	kill	මැරෙනවා	be killed, die
හදනවා	make	හැදෙනවා	be made

73

2.17.4 <u>Complex</u> <u>verbs</u> <u>with</u> ගන්නවා <u>and</u> දෙනවා .

Complex verbs are formed with ගන්නවා and දෙනවා . Examples
appear below.

<u>basic</u> <u>verb</u>		<u>form with</u> ගන්නවා	<u>form with</u> දෙනවා
හදනවා	make	හදාගන්නවා	හදාදෙනවා
හොයනවා	search	හොයාගන්නවා	හොයාදෙනවා
කපනවා	cut	කපාගන්නවා	කපාදෙනවා

There are a limited number of high frequency verbs which show
these patterns. Generally the verb with ගන්නවා means 'do
something for oneself' and the one with දෙනවා 'do something for
others.' Examples:

මම ගෙයක් හදාගත්තා .	I built the house (room) for myself.
වඩුවා ගෙයක් හදාදුන්නා .	The carpenter built (us) a house.

The දෙනවා form may also occur with a preceding participle with
no change in meaning. For example:

වඩුවා ගෙයක් හදලා දුන්නා .	The carpenter built us a house.

Sometimes verbs which are formed in this way have semantically
specialized meanings. For example:

<u>basic</u> <u>verb</u>		<u>derived</u> <u>verb</u>	
කියනවා	say	කියාදෙනවා	explain
බලනවා	see	බලාගන්නවා	look after, care for.

2.17.5 <u>Summary</u> <u>note</u> <u>to</u> <u>the</u> <u>student</u>

The rules for deriving certain types of verbs (causative, passive,
complex) have scarcely been fully explained above. Furthermore,
since many verbs do not show the complete array of forms which
have been discussed, it may not be useful for students to attempt
to generalize the sketchy rules which have been presented. However the information here should demonstrate that there are clusters of verbs which are similar in form and in meaning which can
be remembered as sets.

74

2.18 The clause subordinator කියලා

කියලා is a particle which follows certain types of subordinate
clauses, usually those involving reported speech, ideas or names.
Compare the following:

මම එයාට කිව්වා, 'දොර අරින්න.'   I told him, "open the door."

මම එයාට කිව්වා දොර අරින්න කියලා.   I told him to open the door.

                                               similarly

එයාගෙන් අහන්න, 'නම මොකද්ද?'   Ask him, "what is your name?"

එයාගෙන් අහන්න නම මොකද්ද කියලා.   Ask him what his name is.

This particle also marks the quotation of a name or word. For
example:

තාත්තාගේ තාත්තාට අපි කියන්නේ සීය   We call father's father <u>siiya</u>.
කියලා.
අපි ඒවාට කියන්නේ පොල් අතු කියලා.   We call those things coconut branches

2.19 <u>Nouns derived from verb forms.</u>

One type of verbal noun is formed with the present verbal adjective
plus එක .   Hence, කරන එක , 'the doing.'   These nouns are Class
C nouns (see 1.23).   Example:

එයා කරන එකට මොකද්ද කියන්නේ?   What do you say for what he is
                                            doing?

Such nouns may be based on other adjectival forms of the verb
as well.   For example:

එයා දැන් කරපු එකට මොකද්ද කියන්නේ? What do you say for what he has
                                            just done?

එයා කෙරුව එක ලේසි නෑ.   What he did was not easy.

3. Demonstratives and interrogatives

3.1 The adjectives

Demonstratives and interrogatives fall into sets. The adjective set appears below.

මේ	this, these
අර	that over there, those
ඔය	that near you, those
ඒ	that which we have previously referred to; those
කොයි, මොන	which

These adjectives precede the nouns they modify. For example:

මේ කෙසෙල්ගෙඩි.	These bananas.
අර මහත්තයා.	That gentleman over there.
ඔය ලියකියවිලි.	Those documents near you, with you.
ඒ වැඩ.	That work (we were talking about)
කොයි වැඩ. මොන ලියකියවිලි.	Which work; what documents.

They need not directly precede the noun they modify, however. Other adjectives may intervene. For example:

මේ ලාබ කෙසෙල්ගෙඩි.	These cheap bananas.
අර කොට මහත්තයා.	That short gentleman over there.
ඔය පරන ලියකියවිලි.	Those old documents.
ඒ අලුත් වැඩ.	That new work.
කොයි අලුත් වැඩ. මොන පරන ලියකියවිලි.	What new work; what old documents.

3.2 Pronouns

3.21 The basic set

The demonstratives which appeared in 3.1 may also function as pronouns. For example:

මේ ගමක්	This is a village.
අර වැවක්	That (over there) is a tank.

3.22 The inanimate set

The following words are also pronouns and refer to inanimate nouns.

singular		plural	
මේක	this one	මේවා	these
අරක	that one	අරවා	those
ඕක	that one	ඕවා	those
ඒක	that one	ඒවා	those
මොකක්	what one	මොනවා	what ones
කෝක	which one		

The demonstratives take case endings as follows:

	singular	plural
direct	මේක	මේවා
dative	මේකට	මේවාට
genitive	මේකේ	මේවායේ
instrumental	මේකෙන්	මේවායින්

77

Examples:

මේක පාච්චි කරන්නේ මොකට ද?	What do you use this thing for?
ඒක පාච්චි කරන්නේ මිරිස් අඹරන්න.	You use it to grind chillies.
අරවා පාච්චි කරන්නේ මොකට ද?	What do you use those things for?
ඒවා මෙහෙත් ජාතියක්.	They are a kind of medicine.
පත්තර තුනක් තියෙනවා. ඒවායේ ලංකාවේ හැම පලාතකම ආරංචි තියෙනවා.	There are three newspapers. In them there is news from every part of Sri Lanka.
ඕකට කියන්නේ මොකද්ද?	What do you call that thing near you?
මේකට කියන්නේ මිරිස් ගල කියලා.	For this you say miris gala.

3.33 The animate set

The animate pronominal set is given below.

singular		plural	
මෙයා	this person	මෙයාලා	these people
ඔයා	you	ඔයාලා	you (pl.)
අරයා	that person	අරයාලා	those people
එයා	that person	එයාලා	those people

These are the words which appear most commonly in Sinhala as the equivalents of the English 'he', 'she' and 'they'. As the translations above indicate, the words ඔයා and ඔයාලා serve as second person pronouns.

The demonstrative animate pronouns show the case endings outlined in section 1.2.

The Sinhala word for 'who, what person' is කවුරු . Before ද it is shortened as follows: කවුද . Its case forms are:

direct	කවු(රු)	who
dative	කාට	to whom
genitive	කාගේ	of whom, whose
instrumental	කාගෙන්	by whom

78

With the addition of ත to any of its case forms, කවුරු takes on the meaning 'everybody.'   Examples:

direct	කවුරුත්	everybody
dative	කාටත්	to everybody
genitive	කාගෙත්	of everybody
instrumental	කාගෙනුත්	by, from everybody

3.24 Here and there

Sinhala has the following location sets.

මෙතන	this place, this spot
ඔතන	that place near you
අතන	that place over there
එතන	that place referred to earlier
කොතන	what place
මෙහේ	here
ඔහේ	over there near you
අරහේ	over there, yonder
එහේ	there
කොහේ	where
මෙහා	this direction
එහා	that direction

The words in these sets have case forms as follows:

SAT MAHAL PRASADA, POLONNARUWA

direct	මෙතන	මෙහේ	මෙහා
dative	මෙතන්ට	මෙහේට	මෙහාට
genitive	මෙතන	මෙහේ	මෙහා
instrumental	මෙතනින්	මෙහෙන්	මෙහෙරෙන්

3.25 The quantity set

The quantity set is given below.

මෙච්චර	this much
ඔච්චර	that much
අච්චර	that much
එච්චර	that much
කොච්චර	how much

Examples:

කොච්චර කිරි බොනවා ද?	How much milk will you drink?
මට ඔච්චර එපා.	Not that much for me.
කළගෙඩියක් මෙච්චර ලොකුයි.	A water vessel is this big.
සෙම්බුවක් එච්චර ලොකු නෑ.	A sembuwa is not that big.

3.26   The 'like this ...like that' set

The following words pattern with the demonstratives and interrogatives discussed in the sections above.

මෙහෙම	like this
ඔහොම	like that
අරහෙම	like that
එහෙම	like that
කොහොම	how

81

Examples:

හිරමණයක් පාවිච්චි කරන්නේ කොහොම ද?	In what manner (how) do you use a coconut scraper?
මෝල්ගහෙන් මෙහෙම කොටනවා ද?	Is this how you pound with the pestle?
ඔව්. ඔහොම තමයි.	Yes. Just like that (just as you are doing.)
එහෙම ද?	Is that so? (following a statement of fact.)
එහෙම නෙමෙයි.	It is not like that. (following an inaccurate description of events or procedures.)

3.27 Pronouns: miscellaneous forms

Most of the Sinhala pronouns belong to the demonstrative/interrogative sets. The first person pronouns මම , 'I', and අපි , 'we', are exceptions. They show the following case forms:

direct	මම	I	අපි	we
dative	මට	to me	අපට	to us
genitive	මගේ	my	අපේ	ours
instrumental	මගෙන්	by me	අපෙන්	by us

The reflexive pronoun තමන් , 'his, her own, their own', is also an exception. Its case forms are:

direct	තමන්
dative	තමන්ට
genitive	තමන්ගේ
instrumental	තමන්ගෙන්

Examples:

එයාලා තමන්ගේ කෑම හදාගත්තවා.   They prepare their own food.

එයාලා තමතමන්ගේ කෑම හදාගත්තවා.   They each prepare their own
                                        food.

In the latter example තමතමන් , a reduplicated form of the
reflexive pronoun appears. It has the meaning 'each his own,
each their own.'

3.28 A note on terms of address and reference

The choice of a term of address is a matter which is discussed
in General Conversation. The simple fact is that there is no
neutral second person pronoun which is appropriate for all people
at all times in all places. This helps to explain why the Sinhalese
often avoid second person pronouns entirely and choose such terms
as madam or sir or address people by name or occupational role
instead.

Terms of reference present similar problems in many instances. In
the case of women, for example, the term නෝනා මහත්තය , 'madam',
is only appropriate as a term of reference for those of an
elevated social, educational or occupational station.   Since the
term for woman (ගෑනී) is in its singular form considered insul-
ting, women are generally referred to as 'this person' or 'that
person' (මෙයා and එයා among other terms) and not as 'this woman'
or 'that woman.'   The term ගෑනු , 'women', is not similarly stig-
matized, although in the traditional sectors in the society the
circumlocution බවලත් අය is commonly used. This term literally
means 'those who have received rebirth.' Better educated women
point out that this term is implicitly pejorative, since it reflects
a belief linking demeritorious acts in previous births with being
a woman.

By the same token the term මිනිහා, 'man', though not rude is not
deferential either and is better rendered by English 'guy'. Its
plural, මිනිස්සු , means 'people' not 'men' in the narrow sense. For
the latter the Sinhala is පිරිමි අය , 'men, males, boys.'

In the traditional sectors of the society බයිනඩව and පුරුෂයා , elevated
terms for 'wife' and 'husband' respectively are nearly universally
avoided. Women refer to their husbands by circumlocution. Terms
such as පුතාගේ තාත්තා , '(my) son's father', are commonly used.
Educated people who know English profess to find these habits
quaint but are no more comfortable with the elevated terms. They
sometimes use the English terms instead. Traditional terms for
'wife' include බැඳලා ඉන්න එක්කෙනා, 'married one' and ගෙදර එක්කෙනා ,'the
one in the house.'

83

RUINS OF CIRCULAR RELIC HOUSE AT MEDIRIGIRIYA

4. Postpositions

Postpositions in Sinhala are functionally similar to English prepositions, except that whereas English prepositions occur before the word they govern, Sinhala postpositions occur following the word.   Postpositions occur in construction with nouns, and some occur in construction with other parts of speech as well. When in construction with nouns, many of them govern specific cases, generally the direct case. Examples:

Sinhala	English	Usual case of noun
උඩ	on top of	direct
යට	under	direct
ඉහළ	above	dative/instrumental
පහළ	below	dative/instrumental
ළඟ, ගාව, කිට්ටුව	near	direct
ගැන	about	direct
වගේ	like	direct
විතරක්	only	direct
ඉඳලා	from	genitive
ඉස්සර, ඉස්සෙල්ලා	before	dative/instrumental
පස්සේ	after	dative/instrumental
වැඩියෙ	more than	dative

4.1   වැඩියෙ , 'more than'.

වැඩියෙ, 'more than', occurs with preceding nouns in the dative case to form the equivalent of the English comparative. Examples:

එලවලුවලට වැඩියෙ පලතුරු ගණන්. More than vegetables, fruit is expensive.(fruit is more expensive than vegetables.)

අර ගෙදරට වැඩියෙ මේ ගෙදර ලොකුයි. This house is bigger than that house.

5. Particles

5.1 - ත, 'also, too'

The particle ⁻ත , meaning 'also', is added to words ending in a
vowel. For words ending in a consonant, - උත් is added.

Examples:

අපි අම්මාගේ තාත්තාට කියන්නේ සීය   We call mother's father siiya.
කියලා.
අපි තාත්තාගේ තාත්තාටත් කියන්නේ සීය   We call father's father siiya too.
කියලා.

එයා කන්තෝරුවට ගියා.   He went to the office.

එයාත් කන්තෝරුවට ගියා.   He also went to the office.

බත් දෙන්න.   Give rice.

බතුත් දෙන්න.   Give rice too.

මට ලියුමක් ලැබුනා.   I got a letter.

මටත් ලියුමක් ලැබුනා.   I also got a letter.

5.2 ද..ද, 'or'.

In interrogative sentences ද..ද   means 'or'.

Examples:

මේ පන්තියට උගන්නන්නේ තේන්ථ මහත්තයා   Is it the lady or the gentleman who
ද මහත්තයා ද?   teaches this class?

මගේ ද තේන්ථ මහත්තයාගේ ද?   Mine or the lady's?

මේ කළගෙඩියක් ද මුට්ටියක් ද?   Is this a water vessel or a rice
                                    pot?

ඒක හරි ද වැරදි ද?   Is it right or wrong?

86

SINHALA

5.3 The 'and' particle

There is no single word in Sinhala for 'and' as there is in English. In Sinhala 'and' is expressed by a particle which follows all nouns to be linked.

If the nouns to be linked end in vowels, the 'and' particle takes the shape ඦ . Examples:

පුතායි දුවයි.   The son and the daughter

මහත්තයායි මමයි.   The gentleman and I

If the nouns to be linked end in consonants, the 'and' particle takes the shape උයි . Examples:

බ්‍රවුන් කියලා මහත්තයෙකුයි හේරත් කියලා   A gentleman named Brown and a
මහත්තයෙකුයි.   gentleman named Herath.

හැන්දකුයි පිහියකුයි.   A spoon and a knife.

5.4 The emphasizing particle ඦ .

In equational sentences (the type x is y) with adjectives in the 'y' slot, the emphasizing particle ඦ occurs. Examples:

මේ එලවලු ලාබයි.   These vegetables are cheap.
                                          compare:
මේ ලාබ එලවලු.   These cheap vegetables.
                                          and
මේ එලවලු ලාබ ද?   Are these vegetables cheap?

This particle is also added to definite forms of numerals occuring in sentence final position. Examples:

රාත්තලක් රුපියල් දෙකයි.   Two rupees a pound.

සේරුවක් සත හැත්තෑපහයි.   75¢ a measure.

පැකැට් එකක් එකයි පනහයි. එකක්‍ෟසත   Rs. 1.50 a packet; 50¢ each.
පනහයි.

වේලාව අටයි විස්සයි. වේලාව අටයි.   The time is 8:20; the time is 8:00.

Note that in some quantity phrases such as the last two examples ඦ may appear on two numerals (one of them non-final) in a compound phrase. Such constructions are examples of ඦ as the 'and' particle (see above).

It is also added to other quantity words which occur in sentence final position:

එයාලා බත් කන්නේ දවසට එක සැරයයි.   They eat rice once a day.

වේලාව දැන් අට හමාරයි.   It is 8:30.

සත හැටක් විතරයි.   It is only 60¢.

It may occur with emphasized words in emphatic sentences:

නගුල පාවිච්චි කරන්නේ මෙහෙමයි.   This is how you use the plow.

මම දැන් වැඩ කරන්නේ කොළඹමයි.   It is in Colombo itself that I am now working.

In the environments discussed above, යි does not occur after consonants. Compare:

එළවලු ගණන්.   The vegetables are expensive.
    with
එළවලු ලාබයි.   The vegetables are cheap.

යි may also occur after පුළුවන,'can', and කැමති , 'like', in sentence final position.   Examples:

සිනි දාලා බොන්න කැමතියි.   I like to drink it with sugar.

මට කියාදෙන්න පුළුවනි.   I can explain.

5.5   The emphasizing particles නම් and ම .

The particles නම් and ම may single out a word in the sentence for emphasis.   Examples:

මහත්තයා නම් කන්තෝරුවට ගියා. මම ගියේ නෑ.   It was the gentleman who went to the office. I didn't go.

මට නම් මතක නෑ.   I myself do not remember.

අටටම ආපහු එන්න.   Come back precisely at 8:00.

When ම appears at the end of the sentence it becomes මයි . Examples

මම ඉපදුනේ ලංකාවේමයි.   It was in Sri Lanka itself that I was born.

එයා ආපහු ආවේ අටටමයි.   He came back precisely at 8:00.

88

5.6 The particle හරි.

The particle හරි occurs in the following types of constructions:

a. හරි .... හරි , 'or'.

The word හරි means 'or', or 'either...or', and like the 'and' particle, it follows all words to be linked. For example:

මේ වතුර එන්නේ ඔයකින් හරි, ගඟකින්   This water comes from an oya,
හරි වැවකින් හරි.   from a river or from a tank.

b. හරි   with question words.

   හරි is added to question words to form the following types of new meanings.

කොහේ	where	කොහේ හරි	somewhere or other
කොහොම	how	කොහොම හරි	somehow or other

5.7 The particle වත්

Like හරි the particle වත් is used with question words to form the following types of new meanings.

කොහේ	where	කොහේවත්	anywhere somewhere
කොහොම	how	කොහොමවත්	anyhow somehow

It is also found in constructions which parallel those of හරි ... හරි above.

එයාවත් මමවත් යන්නේ නෑ.   Neither he nor I is going.

6. Numerals and quantity

6.1 Cardinal numerals

Cardinal numerals have both animate and inanimate forms. For example:

නංගිලා තුන් දෙනෙක් ඉන්නවා.   There are three younger sisters.

මම එයාට රුපියල් තුනක් දුන්නා.   I gave him three rupees.

Animate cardinal numerals either modify or substitute for animate nouns. Inanimate numerals either modify or substitute for inanimate nouns. For example:

අක්කලා හතර දෙනයි.   Four older sisters.

හතර දෙනයි.   Four (animate beings).

පෙට්ටි හතරයි.   Four boxes.

හතරයි.   Four (inanimate things).

Both animate and inanimate numerals have definite and indefinite forms. In basic sentence types (that is, non-emphatic sentences) numerals and other quantity words as well generally appear in the indefinite form. When numerals and other quantity words occur as the emphasized items in emphatic sentences or when they are part of a noun phrase which stands along as an utterance, the definite form appears. Compare the following:

වැඩකරයෝ අට දෙනෙක් රැස්වීමට ආවා.   Eight laborers came to the meeting.

රැස්වීමට ආවේ වැඩකරයෝ අට දෙනයි.   It was eight laborers who came to the meeting.

වැඩකරයෝ කීදෙනෙක් ආවා ද?   How many laborers came?

අට දෙනයි.   Eight.

මේ ගමේ ගෙදරවල් පනස් පහක් තියෙනවා.   There are fifty five houses in this village.

ගෙදරවල් කියක් ද?   How many houses are there?

පනස් පහයි.   Fifty-five.

90

When the quantity phrase has a clearly definite meaning, i.e.,
'the laborers' as opposed to 'laborers' or is modified by one
of the demonstratives, the definite form may appear in non-final
position.   For example:

වැඩකාරයෝ අට දෙනා රැස්වීමට ආවා.	The eight laborers came to the meeting.
ඒ අක්කලා හතර දෙනා තවම ගෙදර ඉන්නවා.	Those four older sisters are still at home.

Compare the following:

මහත්තුරු හතර දෙනෙක් කත්තෝරුවේ ඉන්නවා.	There are four gentlemen in the office.
ඒ මහත්තුරු හතර දෙනාම ඉංග්‍රීසි දන්නේ නෑ.	Those very four gentlemen do not know English.

The interrogatives කීයක් , 'how many' (inanimate), and කීදෙනෙක්,
'how many' (animate)', introduce questions concerning quantity.
කොච්චර , 'how much, how many', may be substituted for either,
although it is more common with inanimate subjects. Examples:

කුඹුරුවල ගොවියෝ කීදෙනෙක් වැඩ කරනවා ද?	How many farmers are working in the fields?
ලියකියවිලි කියක් තියෙනවා ද?	How many documents are there?
කොච්චර වේලා යනවා ද?	How much time does it take (go)?

Questions concerning price, age and time are introduced by the
interrogative කීය (ද)   , 'how much'. Examples :

වේලාව කීය ද?	What time is it?
රාත්තලක් කීය ද?	How much is a pound?
වයස කීය ද?	How old are you, i.e., what is the age?

'At what time?' is expressed by කීය in the dative case.

මහත්තයා කීයට ද එන්නේ?	At what time are you coming, sir?

Quotations of time appear in the definite form followed by
the emphasizing particle යි

Examples:

වේලාව කීය ද?	What time is it?
(වේලාව) අටයි.	It is 8:00.
(වේලාව) අටයි විස්සයි.	It is 8:20.
(වේලාව) අට හමාරයි.	It is 8:30.
(වේලාව) දෙකට කාලයි.	It is quarter to 2.

'At a particular time' is expressed with the numeral in the dative case.   Examples:

තත්තෝරුව අරින්නේ කීයට ද?	At what time does the office open?
ඒක අට හමාරට අරිනවා.	It opens at 8:30.
ඒක හතට අරිනවා.	It opens at 7:00.
ඒක අරින්නේ අටට.	It is at 8:00 that it opens.

Prices are generally quoted as follows:

වම්බොටු කීය ද?	How much is eggplant?
රාත්තලක් හැට පහයි.	65¢ a pound.

Amounts of money are commonly quoted in indefinite quantity phrases:

සල්ලි කීයක් දුන්නා ද?	How much money did you pay?
මම රුපියල් හතලිහක් දුන්නා.	I paid Rs. 40.

With the word සැරය , 'time, occurrence', a stem form of the numeral precedes.

එයාලා දවසට දෙ සැරයක් බත් කනවා.	They eat rice twice a day.
යන හැටි එයා කියාදුන්නේ තුන් සැරයි.	He explained how to go three times.

This stem form also appears with ordinal numerals which are discussed below.

Definite and indefinite forms of animate and inanimate numerals appear below.

	Animate		Inanimate	
	Definite	Indefinite	Definite	Indefinite
1	එක්තෙනා	එක්තෙනෙක්	එක	එකක්
2	දෙන්නා	දෙන්නෙක්	දෙක	දෙකක්
3	තුන් දෙනා	තුන් දෙනෙක්	තුන	තුනක්
4	හතර දෙනා	හතර දෙනෙක්	හතර	හතරක්
5	පස් දෙනා	පස් දෙනෙක්	පහ	පහක්
6	හය දෙනා	හය දෙනෙක්	හය	හයක්
7	හත් දෙනා	හත් දෙනෙක්	හත	හතක්
8	අට දෙනා	අට දෙනෙක්	අට	අටක්
9	නම දෙනා	නම දෙනෙක්	නමය	නමයක්
10	දහ දෙනා	දහ දෙනෙක්	දහය	දහයක්
11	එකොලොස් දෙනා	එකොලොස් දෙනෙක්	එකොලහ	එකොලහක්
12	දොලොස් දෙනා	දොලොස් දෙනෙක්	දොලහ	දොලහක්
13	දහතුන් දෙනා	දහතුන් දෙනෙක්	දහතුන	දහතුනක්
14	දාහතර දෙනා	දාහතර දෙනෙක්	දාහතර	දාහතරක්
15	පහලොස් දෙනා	පහලොස් දෙනෙක්	පහලොහ	පහලොහක්
16	දහසය දෙනා	දහසය දෙනෙක්	දහසය	දහසයක්
17	දාහත් දෙනා	දාහත් දෙනෙක්	දාහත	දාහතක්
18	දහඅට දෙනා	දහඅට දෙනෙක්	දහඅට	දහඅටක්
19	දහනම දෙනා	දහනම දෙනෙක්	දහනමය	දහනමයක්
20	විසි දෙනා	විසි දෙනෙක්	විස්ස	විස්සක්

	Animate		Inanimate	
	Definite	Indefinite	Definite	Indefinite
21	විසිඑක් දෙනා	විසිඑක් දෙනෙක්	විසිඑක	විසිඑකක්
22	විසිදෙන්නා	විසිදෙන්නෙක්	විසිදෙක	විසිදෙකක්
23	විසිතුන් දෙනා	විසිතුන් දෙනෙක්	විසිතුන	විසිතුනක්
24	විසිහතර දෙනා	විසිහතර දෙනෙක්	විසිහතර	විසිහතරක්
25	විසිපස් දෙනා	විසිපස් දෙනෙක්	විසිපහ	විසිපහක්
26	විසිහය දෙනා	විසිහය දෙනෙක්	විසිහය	විසිහයක්
27	විසිහත් දෙනා	විසිහත් දෙනෙක්	විසිහත	විසිහතක්
28	විසිඅට දෙනා	විසිඅට දෙනෙක්	විසිඅට	විසිඅටක්
29	විසිනම දෙනා	විසිනම දෙනෙක්	විසිනමය	විසිනමයක්
30	තිස්දෙනා	තිස්දෙනෙක්	තිහ	තිහක්
31	තිස්එක් දෙනා	තිස්එක් දෙනෙක්	තිස්එක	තිස්එකක්
32	තිස්දෙන්නා	තිස්දෙන්නෙක්	තිස්දෙක	තිස්දෙකක්

All other numerals in the thirty series follow the pattern of the twenty series except that තිස් appears instead of විසි

40	හතලිස් දෙනා	හතලිස් දෙනෙක්	හතලිහ	හතලිහක්
41	හතලිස්එක් දෙනා	හතලිස්එක් දෙනෙක්	හතලිස්එක	හතලිස්එකක්
42	හතලිස්දෙන්නා	හතලිස්දෙන්නෙක්	හතලිස්දෙක	හතලිස්දෙකක්

All numerals in the forty series follow the pattern of the twenty series except that හතලිස් appears instead of විසි.

50	පනස්දෙනා	පනස්දෙනෙක්	පනහ	පනහක්
51	පනස්එක් දෙනා	පනස්එක් දෙනෙක්	පනස්එක	පනස්එකක්
52	පනස්දෙන්නා	පනස්දෙන්නෙක්	පනස්දෙක	පනස්දෙකක්

All numerals in the fifty series follow the pattern of the twenty series except that පනස් appears instead of විසි.

94

	Animate		Inanimate	
	Definite	Indefinite	Definite	Indefinite
60	හැටදෙනා	හැටදෙනෙක්	හැට	හැටක්
61	හැටඑක් දෙනා	හැටඑක් දෙනෙක්	හැටඑක	හැටඑකක්
62	හැටදෙන්නා	හැටදෙන්නෙක්	හැටදෙක	හැටදෙකක්

All numerals in the sixty series follow the pattern of the twenty series except that හැට appears instead of විසි.

70	හැත්තෑදෙනා	හැත්තෑදෙනෙක්	හැත්තෑව	හැත්තෑවක්
71	හැත්තෑඑක් දෙනා	හැත්තෑඑක් දෙනෙක්	හැත්තෑඑක	හැත්තෑඑකක්
72	හැත්තෑදෙන්නා	හැත්තෑදෙන්නෙක්	හැත්තෑදෙක	හැත්තෑදෙකක්

All numerals in the seventy series follow the pattern of the twenty series except that හැත්තෑ appears instead of විසි.

80	අසූදෙනා	අසූදෙනෙක්	අසූව	අසූවක්
81	අසූඑක් දෙනා	අසූඑක් දෙන්නෙක්	අසූඑක	අසූඑකක්
82	අසූදෙන්නා	අසූදෙන්නෙක්	අසූදෙක	අසූදෙකක්

All numerals in the eighty series follow the pattern of the twenty series except that අසූ appears instead of විසි.

90	අනූදෙනා	අනූදෙනෙක්	අනූව	අනූවක්
91	අනූඑක් දෙනා	අනූඑක් දෙනෙක්	අනූඑක	අනූඑකක්
92	අනූදෙන්නා	අනූදෙන්නෙක්	අනූදෙක	අනූදෙකක්

All numerals in the ninety series follow the pattern of the twenty series except that අනූ appears instead of විසි.

100	එකසියදෙනා	එකසියදෙනෙක්	එකසිය	එකසියන්
101	එකසියඑක් දෙනා	එකසියඑක් දෙනෙක්	එකසියඑක	එකසියඑකක්

For the rest of the numerals in the 100+ series එකසිය- , '100', is prefixed to the numerals to 99.

RUINS AT YAPAHUVA, 14th CENTURY

Below are the prefixes for the additional hundred series to 1000.

200   දෙසිය

300   තුන්සිය

400   හාරසිය

500   පන්සිය

600   හයසිය

700   හත්සිය

800   අටසිය

900   නමසිය

They precede the numerals to 99 in expressing quantities to 1000.

The stem form for 1000 is එක්දාස් . This is prefixed to the numerals of the 900 series in expressing the years of this century.

එක්දාස් නමසිය විස්සයි.	One thousand nine hundred and twenty.
එක්දාස් නමසිය හැටපහයි.	1965.
එක්දාස් නමසිය හැත්තෑඅටයි.	1978.

To express 'in such and such a year', the final numeral is put in the genitive case and optionally followed by දී, 'during'.

එක්දාස් නමසිය හැටපහේ.	In 1965.
එක්දාස් නමසිය හැත්තෑහතේ දී, මම ලංකාවට ආවා.	I came to Sri Lanka in 1977.
මම ඉපදුනේ එක්දාස් නමසිය හතලිස් හයේ දී.	I was born in 1946.

6.2 Ordinal numerals

Ordinal numerals from 1-10 are given below.

1st   පලවෙනි

2nd   දෙවෙනි

3rd   තුන්වෙනි

4th   හතරවෙනි

5th   පස්වෙනි

6th   හයවෙනි

7th   හත්වෙනි

8th   අටවෙනි

9th   නමවෙනි

10th   දහවෙනි

Ordinal numerals are formed with the stem of the numeral plus වෙනි .
The stem form is the one which precedes දෙනා in animate numerals.
Ordinal numerals precede either animate or inanimate numerals
with no change in form.   Examples:

සැප්තැම්බර් මසේ අටවෙනිදා.	The eighth day of September, i.e., September 8.
අගෝස්තු මසේ විසිඑක්වෙනිදා.	The twenty-first day of August, i.e, August 21.
දෙවෙනි පාර.	The second road.
තුන්වෙනි පුතා.	The third son.

7. Word boundaries

The writing conventions in Sinhala are fairly straightforward in general. Spaces generally appear before and after inflected forms of nouns and verbs as well as before and after other parts of speech such as adjectives, postpositions and adverbs. Conventions differ in some instances, for example, in the addition of some particles to other parts of speech, in writing numerals and in writing compound verbs. For example:

තෑපති තුමා සිංහල දන්නවා ලු.

තෑපති තුමා සිංහල දන්නවාලු.

The ambassador evidently knows Sinhala.

විසි දෙකයි.
විසිදෙකයි.

Twenty-two.

එයාලා කුරක්කන් ගල පාවිච්චි කරනවා.
එයාලා කුරක්කන් ගල පාවිච්චිකරනවා.

They are using the rotary quern.

එයාලා කන්තෝරුවේ වැඩ කරනවා.
එයාලා කන්තෝරුවේ වැඩකරනවා.

They are working in the office.

SIGIRIYA ROCK FORTRESS

99

8. Spelling

Sinhala words are generally spelled as pronounced, but some sounds are represented by more than one letter. For example, න and ණ both represent /n/; ල and ළ both represent /l/ and ලු and ළු both represent /lu/.   Sometimes words are spelled both ways, and sometimes there is a preferred spelling. When in doubt, consult a dictionary. Examples of these particular spelling variations appear below in the place names along two major railway lines.

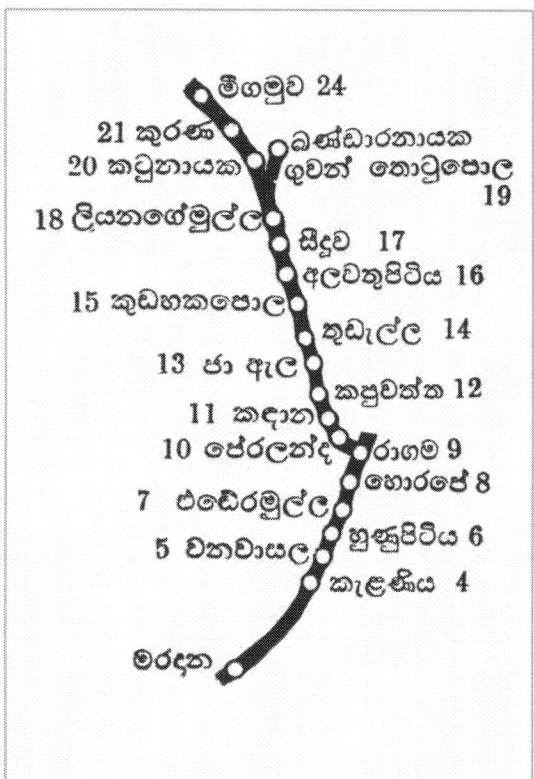
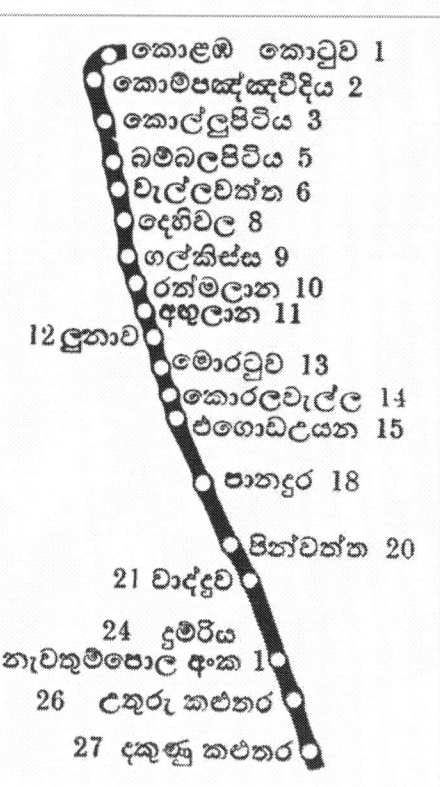

-from Ceylon Government Railway timetable

Numerous other spelling variations occur in Sinhala, mostly in connection with borrowed or learned words. For example, both ශ and ෂ represent /ś/; both ය and ඍ represent /y/ and many words which are pronounced with unaspirated consonants have a correct spelling with letters from the aspirated set. These matters are not treated in any detail here and are best taken up in connection with the study of the conventions of literary Sinhala.

Some differences in spelling of what are essentially the same words do reflect differences in pronunciation and stem from dialect variation within the Sinhala speech community. For example:

කොලොප්පුව, කොලොෂ්ඨුව   stool

අප්පච්චි, අප්පොච්චි   father

පොල් කට්ට, පොල් කටුව   coconut shell

Finally, this may be the place to remind students that Class D nouns such as කාලේ , 'time', which end in ඒ have dictionary entry forms with -ඇය . Hence, කාලය , 'time'. This is a convention from written Sinhala.

9. <u>Style</u> <u>and</u> <u>dialect</u>

This book has reviewed some of the main features of spoken Sinhala structure. Written Sinhala has a different grammatical structure and also, to a large extent, a different and expanded lexicon and is not dealt with here.   This lexicon is borrowed into speech for certain social purposes, for example for speeches or formal lectures on cultural affairs. A student of Sinhala who intends one day to deliver such lectures, then, must master the appropriate formal lexicon.   For a student with such objectives, the study of written Sinhala is an indispensible aid and guide. There are many synopses of written Sinhala structure available, most of them written for speakers of the language. Two which are written for students of Sinhala as a second language are <u>Literary Sinhala: An Introduction</u> (1975) by D.D. DeSaram, and <u>Literary Sinhala</u> (1974) by J.W. Gair and W.S. Karunatilaka (for further details, see the citations in the appended bibliography.)

Most students aim simply to understand the Sinhala which is spoken around them on the routine topics of daily life and work by employ- ees, colleagues and friends. They also aim to communicate with such individuals on the same topics in a stylistically appropriate manner. The style which is presented in this book has been adopted with these ends in mind.   In working through <u>Basic Sinhala</u>, the vocabulary of the students will be expanded considerably beyond the material which is actually presented. It should be kept con- sistent with the style presented here. Substitutions from formal Sinhala should be avoided in favor of words which are in more general use.

The Sinhala speech community is contained within a relatively small geographical area, and the population is highly mobile. Perhaps for these reasons, the community lacks deep dialect divisions. There is variation, of course, and the major differences have been noted at various points above. But for the most part, the Sinhala spoken in one area of Sri Lanka can be easily understood in another.

10. Bibliographical references for the student and the instructor.

The following resources are available for supplementing or continuing basic instruction in Sinhala.

Carter, Charles,   English-Sinhalese Dictionary; Sinhalese
   1936   English Dictionary. 2 volumes. M.D. Gunasena:
   (1965)   Colombo.

This is the basic bilingual dictionary. It has been through several printings since Carter completed it in 1891. It contains a detailed botanical supplement. It is most useful as an aid in decoding since words from the full stylistic range are represented. It is less useful as an aid in encoding since stylistic alternants are not labeled or graded.

Fairbanks, Gordon, J.W. Gair and M. W. S. de Silva, Colloquial
   1968   Sinhalese. 2 volumes. South Asia Program,
                 Cornell University: Ithaca, New York.

This is an introduction to the Sinhala spoken by educated speakers in most normal communication. It contains thirty-six lessons in dialogue format with accompanying grammatical explanations and exercises. The first twelve lessons are in romanization; the remainder are in script. (First volume now unavailable, but likely to be reprinted. Contact South Asia Program, Cornell University.)

Gair, James W. and W.S. Karunatilaka, Literary Sinhala. South
   1974   Asia Program, Cornell University: Ithaca, New York.

This is a basic introduction to written Sinhala for the second language student. Fifteen lessons with texts and grammatical explanations.

Saram, D.D. de, Literary Sinhala: An Introduction. Department
   1975   of Sinhala, University of Sri Lanka, Peradeniya.

This is a basic introduction to written Sinhala for the second
language student. Fifteen lessons with accompanying grammatical
notes and exercises.

☆ U. S. GOVERNMENT PRINTING OFFICE : 1979 O - 301-097 (Book 3)

FOREIGN SERVICE INSTITUTE LANGUAGE PUBLICATIONS
available from
U. S. Government Printing Office, Washington, D. C. 20402
and from
Spoken Language Services, Inc., P. O. Box 783, Ithaca, N. Y. 14850

*(Spoken Language Services agrees to supply the items
below (subject to availability) at current GPO prices
when inquiries indicate that ordering information was
obtained from the Foreign Service Institute.)*

*Amharic	(Units 1-50)	$5.65	Contemporary Cambodian:		
*Amharic	(Units 51-60)	$6.00	Glossary		$4.15
*Saudi Arabic	(Units 1-50)	$3.65	Contemporary Cambodian:		
*Cambodian	(Units 1-45)	$5.05	Grammatical Sketch		$1.50
*Cambodian	(Units 46-90)	$5.25	*Contemporary Cambodian:		
*Cantonese	(Units 1-15)	$4.65	Introduction		$5.40
*Cantonese	(Units 16-30)	$4.65	*Contemporary Cambodian:		
*Chinyanja	(Units 1-63)	$3.70	Land and the Economy		$4.30
*French	(Units 1-12)	$5.75	*Contemporary Cambodian:		
*French	(Units 13-24)	$6.75	Political Institutions		$4.30
*Fula	(Units 1-40)	$5.50	*Contemporary Cambodian:		
*German	(Units 1-12)	$3.45	The Social Institutions		$5.10
*German	(Units 13-24)	$4.35	Dutch Reader		$4.00
*Greek	(Vol. I)	$5.50	*Finnish Graded Reader		$7.00
*Greek	(Vol. II)	$2.70	*French Phonology, Programmed		
*Greek	(Vol. III)	$3.30	Introduction		$5.25
*Hebrew	(Units 1-40)	$6.75	French Phonology, Programmed		
*Hungarian	(Units 1-12)	$4.75	Introduction (Instructor's		
*Hungarian	(Units 13-24)	$5.80	Manual)		$3.00
*Kirundi	(Units 1-30)	$4.80	*German: A Programmed		
*Kituba	(Units 1-35)	$4.15	Introduction		$5.30
*Korean	(Vol. I)	$6.05	Hindi - An Active Introduction		$2.10
*Korean	(Vol. II)	$4.65	*Hungarian Graded Reader		$5.80
Lao	(Vol. I)	$5.00	Indonesian Newspaper Reader		$3.10
Lao	(Vol. II)	$4.35	*Italian (Programmed) Vol. I		$6.70
*Serbo-Croatian	(Units 1-24)	$6.80	Italian, (Programmed) Vol. I		
*Serbo-Croatian	(Units 26-50)	$7.10	Instructor's Manual		$4.05
*Shona	(Units 1-49)	$4.40	*Reading Lao: A Programmed		
*Spanish	(Units 1-15)	$8.45	Introduction		$5.25
*Spanish	(Units 16-30)	$8.00	Communicating in Polish		$3.40
*Spanish	(Units 31-45)	$8.10	*Portuguese: Programmatic		
*Spanish	(Units 46-55)	$5.15	Course, Vol. I		$5.30
*Swahili	(Units 1-150)	$6.75	Portuguese: Programmatic Course		
*Thai	(Units 1-20)	$5.60	(Instructor's Man., Vol. I)		$3.70
*Thai	(Units 21-40)	$4.70	Spoken Brazilian Portuguese		
*Turkish	(Units 1-30)	$5.75	(Units 1-18)		$6.05
Turkish	(Units 31-50)	$5.75	*From Spanish to Portuguese		$1.60
*Twi	(Units 1-20)	$3.00	Russian: An Active Introduction		$2.10
*Vietnamese	(Vol. I)	$3.40	Spanish Programmatic Course		
*Vietnamese	(Vol. II)	$2.95	(Instructor's Manual, Vol. I)		$1.75
*Yoruba	(Units 1-49)	$4.35	*Spanish Programmatic Course		
			(Student Workbook, Vol. I)		$5.20
Adapting and Writing Language			Spanish Programmatic Course		
Lessons		$5.15	(Instructor's Manual, Vol. II)		$1.50
From Eastern to Western Arabic		$ .95	*Spanish Programmatic Course		
*Levantine Arabic: Introduction			(Student Workbook, Vol.II)		$6.65
to Pronunciation		$2.20	*Swahili General Conversation		$1.80
Levantine and Egyptian Arabic			*Swahili Geography		$1.55
Comparative Study		$1.20	Vietnamese Familiarization Crse.		$2.35
*Modern Written Arabic, Vol. I		$4.85	*Yoruba Intermediate Texts		$3.40
Modern Written Arabic, Vol. II		$6.25			
Modern Written Arabic, Vol. III		$7.00			

Supplies of all materials listed are limited, and prices are subject to change without advance notice. Rules require remittance in advance of shipment. Check or money order should be made payable to the agency from which the texts are ordered. Postage stamps and foreign money are not acceptable.

*Tape recordings to accompany these courses are available for purchase from the Sales Branch, National Audiovisual Center (GSA), Washington, D. C. 20409.

Printed in Great
Britain
by Amazon